THERE IT IS

THERE IT IS

Les D. Brown

With an Introduction by Peter Kent

M&S

Canadian Cataloguing in Publication Data

Brown, Les D., 1948-
   There it is: a Canadian in the Vietnam War

ISBN 0-7710-1692-1

1. Brown, Les D., 1948– .   2. Vietnamese Conflict, 1961–1975
– Personal narratives, Canadian.   3. Vietnamese Conflict,
1961–1975 – Participation, Canadian. I.   Title.

DS559.5.B763 2000   959.704'3'092   C00-930071-6

We acknowledge the financial support of the Government of
Canada through the Book Publishing Industry Development
Program for our publishing activities. We further acknowledge the
support of the Canada Council for the Arts and the Ontario Arts
Council for our publishing program.

Though all the events in this book are reported according to the
author's best recollection, some of the names have been changed to
protect the privacy of those mentioned.

Text design by Ingrid Paulson
Typeset in Goudy by M&S, Toronto
Printed and bound in Canada

McClelland & Stewart Inc.
The Canadian Publishers
481 University Ave.
Toronto, Ontario
M5G 2E9

1 2 3 4 5   04 03 02 01 00

To my daughter Jacqueline Susan Joy Brown,
whose birth inspired this book.

CONTENTS

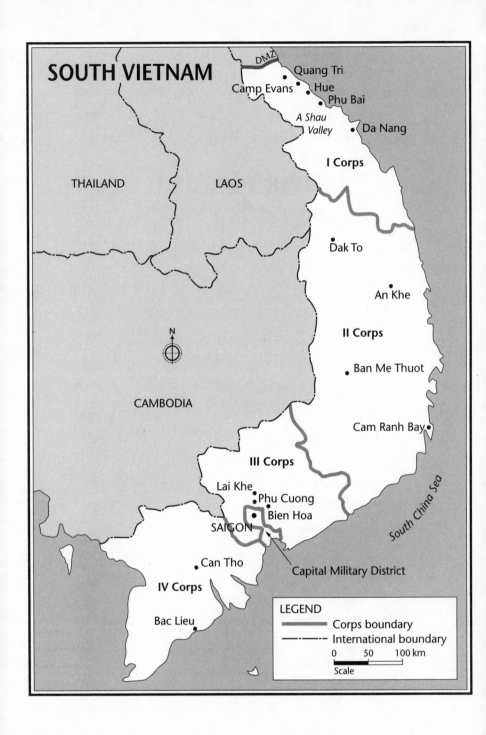

SOUTH VIETNAM

DMZ

Quang Tri

Camp Evans

Hue

Phu Bai

A Shau Valley

Da Nang

I Corps

THAILAND

LAOS

Dak To

An Khe

II Corps

Ban Me Thuot

CAMBODIA

Cam Ranh Bay

III Corps

Lai Khe

Phu Cuong

Bien Hoa

SAIGON

Capital Military District

Can Tho

IV Corps

Bac Lieu

South China Sea

N

LEGEND

Corps boundary

International boundary

0   50   100 km

Scale

Introduction
by Peter Kent

I n the quarter century since the end of the Vietnam War, scores of books have been written dealing with all or part of the conflict. There have been worthy historical treatments, such as *The Ten Thousand Day War: Vietnam, 1945–1975*, by Canadian journalist Michael Maclear, and *Vietnam: A History*, by Stanley Karnow. There have been important insider accounts by those who directed and fought the war; books by Robert S. McNamara, Lyndon Johnson, Vo Nguyen Giap, William C. Westmoreland, and Frank Snepp are required reading for anyone attempting to understand the conflict.

And then there was *Dispatches*, the powerful, first-person narrative of life as a lowly "grunt." Author Michael

Herr eloquently captured the plight of young American men who, both voluntarily and involuntarily, found themselves fighting a war that few ever understood.

Despite the publication of all of these works – whether as a result of inadvertant oversight or political correctness – very little has been written about the thousands of young Canadians who found themselves fighting in Vietnam.

In *There It Is*, one hears echoes of Herr's *Dispatches* as Les Brown examines a spectrum of battlefield emotions: pre-combat fear, post-combat euphoria, the overshadowing preoccupation of personal survival. Brown presents a unique perspective of the war the U.S. couldn't win.

Les Brown wasn't the first Canadian to find himself fighting under the Stars and Stripes. Many thousands of Canadians have borne arms for the U.S. government over the years. Canadians fought in the American Civil War, in the so-called Indian Wars, and in every major U.S. conflict since. Over the course of U.S. history, fifty-three Canadians have been awarded the Medal of Honor, America's highest military award.

In 1970, while Les was struggling to survive ambushes, rockets, mortars, and booby traps in one corner of the Vietnamese battlefield, a fellow citizen, barely a chopper flight away, became the only Canadian to receive the Medal of Honor during the Vietnam War. Peter Lemon, serving as a U.S. Army Ranger, was recognized for conspicuous bravery above and beyond the call of duty. Les never met Peter Lemon during his time in Vietnam. In fact, while he was in Vietnam, Les had no idea just how many fellow Canadians were also part of the massive war effort.

Les has a better idea today, though he still can't know for sure. There are no official figures on the number of Canadian men – and women – who served in Vietnam in the various branches of the U.S. military. Estimates range from five or six thousand to more than fifty thousand. Veterans and historians attribute that broad range to Pentagon priorities in the 1960s, priorities skewed more to delivering fresh troops to a widening war than to maintaining detailed, accurate records of where they came from.

For Canadians, there were two routes into the U.S. forces – as conscripts or as volunteers.

Many of the Canadians who were drafted because they were living in the United States have been found to have been listed in Pentagon records as Americans, simply on account of their residence and because of bureaucratic assumptions. Similarly, many Canadians who volunteered, making their way to the closest U.S. border town to enlist, were misregistered because of their temporary local accommodations.

A spokesman for the U.S. defence department, quoted in a January 1985 New York Times article about Canadian volunteers, said that no numbers could be confirmed because the records of soldiers who served in Vietnam had been "retired." A Canadian government official quoted in the same story doubted that more than five thousand Canadians served in Vietnam.

Don Winrow, president of the London, Ontario, branch of the Vietnam Veterans' Association, believes some forty thousand Canadian citizens served in the U.S. forces during the war. On the other hand, Woody Carmack of Maple Ridge, B.C., the president of the Vietnam Veterans of Canada, puts the number somewhat lower, at twenty to thirty thousand. This is the estimate favoured by many U.S. veterans' organizations. Some American vets, still resentful of draft dodgers, use the figure to draw a parallel between the number of Canadians who served in Vietnam and the number of U.S. citizens who fled to Canada to avoid service.

Carmack says his estimate is supported by data from the U.S. Immigration Service in the mid-1980s that was drawn from analysis of veteran benefits claims. He says the same survey fixes the number of Canadians killed in combat in Vietnam at 111 – their names added to the legions of foreign soldiers who have died in Vietnam over the centuries.

*   *   *

Vietnam, a tiny S-shaped country, barely the size of Newfoundland, has survived some of history's most powerful foreign armies – all intent on exploiting its abundant natural resources or its strategic location on the

South China Sea. To properly understand the twentieth-century conflict in which Les Brown found himself, one must recognize the French colonial oppression that began in the seventeenth century.

First came Jesuit priests sent to save pagan souls in what Europeans then called Indochina. The missionaries were soon followed by traders and settlers. Vietnamese nationalists resisted the gradual colonialization with increasing violence that eventually developed into open warfare. In 1859, the French Foreign Legion was dispatched to contain the hostilities, and in 1861, a French admiral officially proclaimed the seizure of Indochina for France.

Vietnamese nationalists continued to resist through the century, though, developing guerilla tactics that would be used in a succession of conflicts into the 1900s. The French fought fire with fire, imprisoning, torturing, and guillotining thousands of guerillas and their perceived supporters.

There was a resurgence of Vietnamese nationalism when World War I focused French attention on home battlefields. Religious sects such as the Cao Dai were created to foment anti-French attitudes. Political parties such as the Dai Viets were founded to challenge colonial institutions. And, in the wake of the Russian Revolution, some nationalists saw strength in communism. Secret cells were created among the three nationalist groupings, and by the 1930s, the French were again confronted regularly by open rebellion.

The French responded as they had decades before, with reprisal attacks, arrests, torture, executions, and deportations. The repression only deepened the commitment of an emerging group of communist leaders. When Japanese troops occupied Vietnam in 1940, aided by collaborationist French officials, one of those fiercely committed communists appealed to all nationalist groups to "rise up and unite with the people" to throw out all foreign armies.

That fifty-year-old revolutionary, born Nguyen That Thanh, would become known to the world by his *nom de guerre*, Ho Chi Minh (Vietnamese for "He who enlightens"). And the colleague Ho chose to lead the First Armed Propaganda Detachment, Vo Nguyen Giap, would go into the military history books as a master of unconventional warfare. By the end of World War II, the successes of Ho Chi Minh's poorly equipped Viet Minh guerilla army against superior Japanese forces won recognition among Allied intelligence organizations.

Records of the American OSS, forerunner to the CIA, concluded that Ho was not a "hardened communist," that his ultimate goal was to attain American support for the cause of a free Vietnam, and that his nationalist ambitions did not conflict with American policy in the region.

President Roosevelt believed – and attempted to convince his Allied counterparts – that it would be a mistake to free the people of South-East Asia from the

Japanese only to return them to colonial domination. In fact, as early as 1943, Roosevelt was quoted by OSS operative Major Archimedes Patti as saying, "Don't think for a moment that Americans would be dying in the Pacific if it hadn't been for the short-sighted greed of the French and British and Dutch." Roosevelt's successor also favoured a postwar end to French colonial control of Indochina, but the war ended before Truman could lay the diplomatic groundwork to fulfill Roosevelt's dream.

By May 1945, Ho Chi Minh's guerillas, armed with weapons provided by the OSS, were racking up consistent victories against the Japanese and began to establish authority among rural Vietnamese. Those successes alarmed French military commanders who were assuming they would re-establish colonial control of Hanoi as the Japanese withdrew. Japan's sudden capitulation after the detonation of atomic bombs over Hiroshima and Nagasaki created a vacuum in the Vietnamese capital that both the Viet Minh and the French rushed to fill. Ho's forces won the race, and on September 2, 1945, Ho Chi Minh proclaimed the independence of the Democratic Republic of Vietnam.

As a new national flag – red with a single gold star – waved in the wind, a squadron of American fighter aircraft made a ceremonial fly-past. Despite the aerial tribute and the salutes of the sprinkling of American officers on the ground, Washington withheld official recognition of Ho's claimed independence. So did the other signatories to the Potsdam Agreement, the document that divided postwar territorial responsibilities.

While the Great Powers pondered their respective places and diplomatic priorities on the postwar landscape, Ho's path to independence became cluttered and complicated. He claimed the independence of all of Vietnam, but the Potsdam document gave Britain authority over the southern half. Britain reached a side agreement with France returning administration of the zone to the French.

In the North, Ho found that though his forces controlled Hanoi, the countryside was in widening chaos. Disarmed Japanese troops awaiting transportation home were a problem, and two hundred thousand nationalist Chinese troops that had been part of the Allied liberation force were breaking down into rampaging mobs of looters.

A series of complicated side deals were negotiated which led to an Allied compromise offer to Ho. The marauding Chinese "liberators" would be removed if a limited number of French troops were allowed back into the North to maintain order. France pledged to withdraw those troops gradually if the Viet Minh promised not to engage in guerilla activity in the South. The deal did lead to the departure of the nationalist Chinese troops, but within a year, hardliners in the Viet Minh were urging that the French occupation forces leave. Meanwhile, French generals had convinced a new generation of politicians in Paris that all of Indochina should be reclaimed.

French forces retook Haiphong and Hanoi. Ho Chi Minh's Viet Minh forces withdrew to the countryside. For eight years, the French fought an increasingly defensive war to hold their colony. But the Viet Minh persisted and, in May 1954, prevailed in the final battle at Dien Bien Phu.

During the fifty-five-day siege of their garrison 170 miles northwest of Hanoi, the French lost three thousand men. At least as many were permanently disabled. The Viet Minh triumph came at great cost: an estimated eight thousand were killed. However, they had won a great victory, which would provide inspiration over the next two, far more bloody decades.

The new realities presented by the Viet Minh victory were formally recognized at an international conference in Geneva. In the end the Great Powers agreed to a temporary partition of Vietnam at the same mid-point that had been established after World War II. Ho's government agreed to allow a three-month period in which Vietnamese could decide which side they would live on. (More than eight hundred thousand Northerners, mostly Catholics, moved to the South. Fewer than 10 per cent of that number moved north.) France agreed to withdraw all troops from the North and the South within a year, and all sides agreed that free and fair, internationally supervised elections on reunification should be held within two years. They were never held.

In the North, the communists, supported by the Soviet Union, imposed ideological reforms that allowed no room for dissent. Landlords who refused to contribute their land to communes were executed as counter-revolutionaries. Disruptions in food production caused by land reform led to famine.

In the South, a diminutive mandarin from Hue named Ngo Dinh Diem manoeuvred his way into power with a little help from American friends in the CIA. The United States had moved quickly to influence how the vacuum created by the departure of the French would be filled.

In January 1957, the International Control Commission, made up of observers from Canada, Poland, and India, concluded in an official report that neither North nor South Vietnam had fulfilled the central terms of the 1954 Geneva Peace Accords. A Canadian ICC observer said the commission had been ineffective from its inception because of an absence of any spirit of détente between the two sides. The stage was set for widening conflict.

In Washington, the Eisenhower administration became increasingly preoccupied with the ominous "domino theory," which predicted that, if South Vietnam were to fall to the communists, countries down the sub-continent would follow, eventually threatening the Philippines and perhaps even Australia and New Zealand. Despite abundant evidence that Diem was bent on establishing a quasi-monarchy by brutally repressive and corrupt means, the Eisenhower administration justified continued support as a price of defending freedom against the spectre of creeping communism.

By the time John F. Kennedy was sworn into office in 1961, Diem had lost domestic popular support, many of his generals were grumbling about his corrupt leadership, and guerilla activity was on the rise. President Kennedy and his new secretary of defence, Robert S. McNamara, agonized over conflicting advice from military and political advisors at home and in Vietnam. Their considerations were made no easier after the humiliating failure of the U.S.-backed counter-revolutionary invasion of Cuba. Without enthusiasm, Kennedy picked up where Eisenhower had left off. The number of U.S. military "advisors" and "support staff" in Vietnam steadily increased.

When Buddhist monks committed a series of fiery suicides in Saigon to protest injustices by the Diem regime, the Kennedy administration tried to force reforms by threatening to withdraw economic and military support. Diem ignored Washington.

U.S. diplomats and CIA operatives began looking for alternatives. Robert McNamara, writing more than three decades later in his book *In Retrospect: The Tragedy and Lessons of Vietnam*, said Kennedy ordered that the United States should "not take any initiative to encourage actively a change in government." But, by October 1963, South Vietnamese generals were convinced – by a series of diplomatic nudges and winks – that Washington would not oppose a coup d'état.

On October 31, those generals acted. Vietnamese troops seized key installations. President Diem and his brother Ngo Dinh Nhu, supported by the presidential guard, held out for three days before being captured and executed in the back of an armoured personnel carrier.

McNamara remembers that word of Diem's death "shook President Kennedy profoundly." Just as distressing was the "power vacuum" the U.S. now faced in Vietnam. Kennedy didn't get a chance to adjust his foreign policy to the new realities. Three weeks later he, too, fell to an assassin's bullets.

Robert McNamara – again with the benefit of three decades of hindsight – says he believes that, had Kennedy lived, "he would have pulled the United States out of Vietnam." McNamara writes: "He would have concluded that the South Vietnamese were incapable of defending themselves, and that Saigon's grave political weaknesses made it unwise to try to offset the limitations of South Vietnamese forces by sending U.S. combat troops on a large scale."

In the dark days of November and December 1963, there was no time for thoughtful reflection. Lyndon Johnson, the vice-president no one had ever expected to be president, inherited life and death issues in Vietnam that could not wait. Before Kennedy had even been buried, Johnson announced that American aid to the military junta that now controlled South Vietnam would continue. In secret cabinet meetings, McNamara remembers, the instructions on Vietnam were, "Win."

Within months, the joint chiefs of staff were urging aggressive measures to counter communist gains. By mid-1964, Johnson had authorized a variety of secret missions involving air raids, shelling, kidnapping, and assassinations. And then there was the controversial favour requested of Canada.

In a chapter of the war still debated among historians, Johnson authorized Secretary of State Dean Rusk to ask Canadian Prime Minister Lester Pearson to send an emissary to Hanoi with an ultimatum for the North Vietnamese. Pearson reluctantly agreed.

Very little detail of the secret mission was put on paper. It is impossible to document whether Canada's senior ICC delegate, James Blair Seaborn, was actually asked to convey a nuclear threat to North Vietnam. But Pentagon principals – including Daniel Ellsberg, who was later to leak the Pentagon Papers as a whistle-blowing protest of the United States' conduct of the war – referred to Seaborn's trip as a "carrot and stick" operation.

Whatever the specific messages Seaborn delivered to North Vietnam's Premier Pham Van Dong, communist guerilla activity in the South continued and intensified. By the spring of 1965, Johnson, his diplomats, spies, and generals agreed it was time to support South Vietnamese forces with U.S. ground troops. Thirty-five hundred combat troops came ashore on the sparkling white beaches of Da Nang. Within six weeks there were eighty-two thousand. By mid-1966 three hundred thousand American service personnel were deployed throughout the South. By 1967, the number had soared to more than half a million.

Almost three million allied troops were to rotate through South Vietnam, including ninety thousand so-called Free World troops. Canada passed on Washington's invitation to help in the fight against communist expansionism, but Australia, New Zealand, South Korea, Thailand, and the Philippines did send combat forces. Then, on January 31, 1968 – the beginning of Tet, the Chinese New Year – North Vietnam launched the massive offensive that threw South Vietnam into bloody chaos, shook the Johnson administration, and brought anti-war sentiment among the American public to a boil. Across Vietnam, from Saigon to the smallest provincial capital, Vietcong guerillas and units of the North Vietnamese regular army mounted intense, coordinated attacks.

It took five days of often desperate fighting for U.S. forces to regain the upper hand. North Vietnamese troops held portions of the ancient imperial capital of Hue for a full month despite furious counterattacks by U.S. ground and air forces.

Night after night, U.S. network newscasts were dominated by images of American troops bloodied, confused, and, despite individual acts of heroism, increasingly demoralized. History's first television war revealed the most powerful military force in history being stalemated by troops who often rode to battle on bicycles.

President Johnson announced he wouldn't seek re-election. Richard Nixon won the White House after promising Americans he would bring the country's young men home after achieving "peace with honour."

By the time Les Brown arrived in Vietnam, the American politicians, bureaucrats, generals, and spies who were conducting the war knew it was a losing effort. Nixon favoured continuing the conflict while reducing the number of American ground troops. He believed heavy air strikes and battlefield stalemate would eventually force North Vietnam to agree to a negotiated peace that would allow South Vietnam to remain a separate, "democratic" entity.

Nixon would be proved as wrong as the host of foreign leaders who had tried to bend Vietnam to their will over more than two thousand years. The promise of "peace with honour" was never fulfilled.

The war would drag on for another six years. U.S. bombing would intensify even as America talked peace in Paris with the North Vietnamese. The two principal negotiators for the warring countries, Henry Kissinger and Le Duc Tho, would receive the Nobel Peace Prize. Ho Chi Minh would die of a heart attack. Despite American hopes for a self-destructive power struggle within the communist leadership, Ho's comrades would fight on, united, toward completion of his life-long quest to restore the "precarious tradition of unity." Canadian peacekeepers would serve briefly on a new International Supervisory Force, but would withdraw when it was clear that neither side was respecting the so-called truce.

Finally, in the spring of 1975, the U.S. Congress cut off all economic and military support to the Saigon regime. The South Vietnamese military collapsed with breathtaking speed as Northern troops marched, virtually unopposed, on Saigon.

A massive airlift removed the last U.S. ambassador, his staff, an assortment of aid workers, CIA operatives, military advisors, journalists, and thousands of South Vietnamese who had served the allied war effort. In all, more than seven thousand were airlifted out of Saigon on the final day of the war.

And, on May Day 1975, almost twenty-one years to the day after Ho's forces defeated the French at Dien Bien Phu, a North Vietnamese tank would burst through the wrought iron gates of the Presidential Palace in Saigon. The flag of victory would be raised, signalling to the world fulfillment of Ho Chi Minh's dream, proclaiming, in his name, Vietnam united.

But all of that was yet to come, on the October day in 1969 when Les Brown arrived in Vietnam.

1. THE DRAFT

Surfing trip, 1968.

remember the first time I walked point. I had recently arrived in-country and had linked up with my company on Firebase "Lorraine" in III Corps. We were now on the move; my squad had point and the going was tough. Williams, the pointman, had opted to hump into a thick batch of bamboo in order to reduce the risk of being seen by the enemy. Exhausted from the exertion required to hack his way through, he sent word back to the squad leader asking for a replacement and I got volunteered.

I had been following behind, busy adjusting to the heat and the eighty pounds of crap on my back. I was a new guy and was so overwhelmed by it all that having me walk point seemed absurd. I stumbled up front, barely able to stand under the weight of my ruck. Williams handed me his machete and grinned, knowing I was not yet ready for point. I stood there trying to figure out how to hold my weapon and swing a machete at the same time. I had no idea what to do.

Holding my M-16 in my left hand, and the machete in my right, I began to hack. One hack, two hacks, then *clang*, as the blade of the machete met the barrel of my weapon. If the enemy hadn't known man was in the jungle, he knew now. I continued my hacking and stumbled forward about one metre. The going was extremely tough, and I turned to look at my slack man, Williams, with pleading eyes. He merely glanced in the direction of travel, and I went back to my new-guy hacking. My fatigues became completely soaked, as rivers of sweat ran down my face and stung my eyes, blurring my vision. In a matter of minutes I was spent, barely able to stand, let alone chop my way through. My debut as pointman was over. Williams returned to the point position without being ordered to do so. I resumed my stumbling behind the squad's radio telephone operator, and the platoon moved on slowly.

When I look back on this incident, I believe it was my welcoming to the infantry. You're a grunt now, the others were telling me, start suffering along with us. A grunt's discomfort is continual, unless it's interrupted by being blown away. And once a grunt, always a grunt.

In fact, the word grunt itself is special to me. I get angry when people use it in a derogatory way to describe a low-level worker. In my mind, the word is reserved for usage by grunts only, to refer affectionately to one another. The same goes for "pointman." Today, the term is used in politics or business to describe someone leading a new venture, when in reality, a pointman is the grunt who walks point, up front, the one most likely to trip a booby trap or walk into an ambush. The pointman is the eyes of the platoon simply because he gets there first.

By the time I arrived in the field in Vietnam, I had had a total of five months in the U.S. Army. I had been drafted and I did not want to be there. As a draftee, I instinctively never fully committed myself to the U.S. Army or its mission in Vietnam. I simply hoped I would do my required two years' active duty, somehow slip through the cracks, and resume my life in California.

* * *

It was spring of 1968, and I was working in Canoga Park, California, as a mechanic. My local draft board in North Hollywood had seen fit to classify me the dreaded 1-A, highly draftable. I was a Canadian citizen – my family had moved to Los Angeles in 1957 when I was eight – and I naively thought I had my way out. I appealed their decision, but the draft board politely informed me that as a permanent resident, I was required to fulfill my military duty.

By this time, Vietnam had become an unpopular war. The Tet offensive of 1968 had occurred and I and the rest of America had watched on television as events were reported. Every major city and U.S. installation had been attacked simultaneously by large-scale units of enemy soldiers. Up until then, we had been told the enemy consisted of small bands of dissident guerillas. The visual dispatches from Vietnam contributed greatly to the turning of the tide of support for the war.

A coworker of mine was also a Canadian and of draftable age, and we talked about how it would be such a simple solution to return to Canada. The talk eventually turned into a plan and we left in the early summer. My mother was very happy, as she already had one son in Vietnam to worry about. My brother, Ken, had enlisted in the Navy shortly after his high school graduation. He was serving on the flight deck of an aircraft carrier off the coast of Vietnam.

My friend and I stayed with my grandparents in Wakefield, Quebec. I loved being back, the place was my childhood paradise. We went to work for a local farmer who was deep into the hay harvest season and needed help. The pay was one dollar an hour, lunch included. Money was tight, but with free room and board at my grandparents', the scene was manageable.

As the summer slipped by, I discovered something I had not anticipated. I was homesick for Los Angeles. I missed surfing, I missed my '47 Chevrolet Woody, I missed my family, and I really missed my girlfriend, Nancy, who would not leave L.A. to be with me. My buddy also felt homesick, and we confided in each other that we felt a little out of place. We packed the car and headed for home knowing our mutual problem had not disappeared during our draft-avoiding hiatus. We both were rehired at our old jobs, no questions asked, and I resumed my status with my girlfriend.

Looking for another way out of the draft, I registered that fall at L.A. Valley College. I studied Police Science – an old friend had told me that the program was easy, easy enough to maintain the "B" average necessary to qualify for a deferment – but my heart wasn't in it. Eventually, I dropped out. I knew that my draft letter would soon be coming.

* * *

I detested the thought of being in the military. I was unable to express to myself what I felt was wrong with the war, but I was suspicious enough to know I did not want to be involved. All around it was love, peace, and groovy days and that made more sense to me. My early religious upbringing in the United Church of Canada had stuck with me and I sincerely believed that no man had the right to kill another.

There were thousands of ways to avoid service, though none sounded too good to me. I mentally dismissed all the self-mutilation techniques I'd heard about; I couldn't whack off my trigger finger with an axe as others had done. Jail didn't sound too appealing either. I didn't want to commit a crime to obtain a felony record, which would make me undesirable for military service. This was the out for my Canadian travelling partner. He had committed a residential burglary, been arrested and convicted and thus deemed undesirable. I envied him, but was unwilling to be dishonest to avoid service.

Around this time, I had a conversation with my father concerning my feelings about going to Vietnam. He said to me, "If you're good enough to live in this country, then you're good enough to fight for it." My dad was a vet of the big one, World War II. He had lied about his age, and had prematurely enlisted in the Canadian Army. My dad had served in Africa as a dispatch rider running messages via motorcycle, but it was in Sicily that he was captured by the Germans. He had scars on both lower legs from shrapnel wounds he received when he was blown off his motorcycle in a German ambush. He spent two years in various German prisoner-of-war camps before the final victory of the Allies. He spoke very little of his experiences, so much was left to my imagination.

I'll never know to what extent my father's past and his words influenced me, but how could they not? When I was growing up everybody's father was a World War II vet. In school, in church, in Scouts, at the supermarket, everywhere, we, the boomers, were in the presence of the victors. They had saved the world and had earned the right to bark orders and influence us hippies, and we were grateful for their sacrifices. Though I have always minimized his influence on my decision to go to Vietnam, years later, when it was common to speak out against the war, my dad would express regret for any part he played in that decision.

Before allowing myself to be drafted, I went to recruiter row on Brand Boulevard in San Fernando. Each branch of service had a recruiting office there. I already knew that to enlist in the Navy, Air Force, or Marines would mean four long years in the military. I was already leaning towards waiting for the draft, which demanded only two years' active duty. (Two years' active duty included six months of training, a one-year tour in Vietnam, and six months served back in the States.) The trade-off was that if you enlisted, you had a choice of military occupational specialty. If you were drafted, you had no choice. Not wanting to serve at all, two years made more sense to me because I naively thought they'd never put a guy like me in an actual combat situation. I spoke with the Air Force recruiter who promised me, because of my police science background, that I could serve in the Air Police. I thought, "How generous, four years of guarding gates. Thanks a lot, Sarge."

One afternoon, soon after my visit to San Fernando, I returned home from a day out with Nancy to find my draft notice on the kitchen table. I was to report to the induction centre in downtown Los Angeles 13 May 69. I had eight weeks to decide what to do. My mother pleaded for my return to Canada, stating that the war was immoral, and offering me a few hundred dollars she'd saved so I could leave. My father, still not convinced, remained silent, but I interpreted his silence to mean "do the right thing, son."

For a while, I started planning a return trip to Canada. I installed a new motor in the Woody, bought new tires, and prepared to leave. If questioned at the border, I planned to say I was visiting relatives before my induction. I began to lose my resolve, however, and I kept putting off my departure. For reasons that still evade and anger me, I cancelled my trip and waited for my induction date to arrive.

* * *

It did, of course, and on 13 May 69 Nancy dropped me off outside the induction centre. Inside, it was a scene right out of *Alice's Restaurant* complete with the group "W" bench. It was a very busy place, draftees and enlisted alike were being processed for all service branches. All around, it was hurry up and wait. While I visited a nearby washroom, a Marine sergeant had come in and asked for draftee volunteers for the Marine Corps. The Marines demonstrated their typical one-upmanship by serving thirteen-month tours in Vietnam while all other branches served one-year tours. Not one single draftee had volunteered, so the sergeant had indiscriminately picked thirteen draftees for the Marines. As I re-entered the room, I heard loud sob-like pleading from one poor guy who had been selected. He was begging to be allowed to just go in the Army with the rest of us. The sergeant barked, "Shut up, puke, you're a Marine now." I shudder to think of their treatment as draftees in the normally all-volunteer Marines and was grateful I hadn't been in the room.

It was quite a gathering of draftees; every race and background seemed to be represented. Some were still hoping to get out at this last stop before boot camp. Some had obviously starved themselves to appear unfit for service; others were so unwashed, the stench was overwhelming. There were drunken guys and guys high on heroin, pot, LSD, and probably every legal and illegal drug known to mankind. I didn't hear of anybody not making the grade. They took all of us.

The last step in our processing was the "swearing-in ceremony." We were ushered into a large official-looking

blue room. Once sworn in, we would be in our respective branches of service. As a Canadian permanent resident, I was deemed to be a "legal alien" and was required
to take a different oath from the other inductees. I reluctantly complied.

I was stressing big-time. We loaded onto awaiting
buses and departed for basic training at Fort Ord,
California. I felt very alone, alienated and foreign; this
couldn't be happening to me. I was already angry and
disappointed with myself for allowing this to happen,
emotions that would be with me in varying degrees for
the rest of my life. From then on, any resistance I had
left would have to be demonstrated from within the
system. I was now property of the U.S. Army.

2. BASIC TRAINING

Nancy and me on visitation day, Fort Ord.

The horror stories of boot camp that circulate are, no doubt, based in truth, but many I've heard have been obviously exaggerated to shock those who never experienced what the U.S. Army calls Basic Combat Training. By the time I arrived at Fort Ord, California, the system of soldier manufacturing was well oiled, very efficient, and appeared to us trainees to almost run itself. As recruits, we were maggots, naturally, but the vibe I sensed was one of fuck with 'em enough to get their attention but not so much as to cause an uprising. That fine line between compliance and revolt is one the Army was expert at maintaining and I am still in awe of how they managed it. As recruits, we quickly learned to go along to get along and most of us did just that. Shortly into our training, I sensed that although we would be very busy, lonely, dirty, exhausted, isolated, uncomfortable, deprived, hungry, thirsty, horny, depressed, and full of self-pity, nobody would actually hurt us.

A few weeks into our training cycle, I received a letter from my mother. She said that an official team of investigators from some agency had been snooping around our neighbourhood asking people questions about my character. I would later learn that all aliens were checked out in this manner, I guess to ensure we weren't pinko infiltrators or degenerates of questionable character. After all, we were aliens, God knows what we were really up to. Shortly after that, I was approached by a company clerk. He said he had documents that I had to sign because I was a Canadian in the U.S. Army. I was immediately suspicious and asked him what these papers were and what they meant. The clerk barked in the best drill-instructor voice he could muster, "Brown, sign the papers and shut the fuck up." He was a private, and I was just a trainee, so I reluctantly signed the documents. To this day, I have no idea what I actually signed, but in my readings over the years, I discovered that aliens were required to sign waivers before being sent into a combat zone. I never *knowingly* signed such a waiver.

At this time, I was frantically hoping to get a non-combat role. The Army had not yet informed us of our military occupation specialties (MOS), but we all knew Eleven Bravo to be the dreaded designation for the infantry. At the reception centre, before being assigned to our training company, we had been bombarded with testing. Tests of every imaginable type were administered, so the Army, in its infinite wisdom, would know who was best suited for what. Some questions were asked in several different ways and I, having had honesty drilled into me all my life, answered truthfully. I should have fudged when they asked do you like camping, or do you believe in teamwork, or do you support the U.S. government. I was incapable of lying. Besides, I believed what I'd been taught: good things come to good people. I believed myself to be intelligent and hard-working, and because I was at least partially college-educated, I believed I could probably do most for the Army as a clerk. So naturally, when they administered the typing test, I volunteered. I figured this could be my ticket to clerical heaven, even though I had not typed a word since junior high school. I was a little rusty to say the least, and failed miserably. I accepted the defeat and started dreaming up other possible slots for myself.

A few years before, I had driven a truck part-time for my father for his sewing contract business. I had also driven a bobtail dual-wheel hay truck for the farmer in Wakefield the previous summer. On the form asking about truck driver skills, I had indicated "yes." The Army, again in its infinite wisdom, named me company driver.

By getting this job, I managed to escape numerous long humps with the rest of the company. I had to drive the crash truck picking up the heat-stroke victims and delivering chow. I enjoyed driving the big goofy deuce-and-a-half and figured that, for sure, the Army would need me in the future as a truck driver. Unfortunately, this would not be in the cards.

Even as company driver, I still got ample practice at drill, marching, M-14 weapon training, and all the Army stuff you'd expect. One aspect of training still haunts me from time to time. Marches, or forced marches, as they were referred to, were always conducted in a highly military manner which meant we all had to stay in step. In order to achieve this, the drill instructors would call cadence. One "song" in particular that still comes back to me – though I wish it wouldn't – went like this:

> I wanna be an Airborne Ranger
> I wanna lead a life of danger
> I wanna go to Veeyetnam
> I wanna kill some Veeyetcong

These cadence calls were delivered in a monotonous, hypnotic way that we, of course, repeated back to the DIs, embedding them in our brains forever. An hypnotic trance-like state was easy enough for the DIs to manage with all that melodic marching, lots of fatigue, and hours of repetitive drill.

* * *

As a soldier you had a serial number, two letters followed by a series of digits, which told your story. RA stood for Regular Army and meant that you had enlisted. Even at this early date, RAs were showing signs of superior adaptability as compared to the draftees. They had enlisted, after all, and could not blame the Army for their current situation. The RAs had also been promised their MOS by the recruiters. Many were non-combative.

NG stood for National Guard, and this meant you were one of the lucky ones. Unless activated later on, you would face only six months' active duty, and five and a half years' reserve duty. NGs proved to be some of the most annoying recruits around, due to their constant smiling and their prodding of others to shape up. They knew Vietnam was unlikely to happen to them, and they could afford to be cocky. Years later, I would wonder if any of our NGs were involved in the Kent State murders of four university students engaged in an anti-war protest.

Then there were, of course, us draftees. Our serial numbers started with the letters US, which I always assumed stood for United States, though I never knew for sure. When talking to someone new, you would exchange names and ask a two-letter question: US? If the guy answered, "Fuck, yeah," then you knew he was a cool dude because he hated the mother-fuckin' military establishment as much as you did. We US recruits were still waiting to find out what our MOSs would be.

Life at close quarters with lots of other guys is not the most desirable way to live, but there is still life. Strong friendships were formed and cliques of like-thinkers emerged. Recruits bitched, chided, teased and rah-rahrahed one another. One guy that bunked adjacent to me was a very effeminate guy named Nelson. We became friends, perhaps because he sensed I was non-aggressive and approachable. He spoke often of his mother, and he never made a sexual advance. Nelson was a recycle, which meant he was doing basic training over again. During his first go around, he had become totally despondent and had attempted suicide. He never discussed his suicide attempt and I didn't ask. Nelson graduated with the rest of the company. I don't know what became of him, but I hope he survived and flourished.

We had another recycle in our barracks, though I never knew the reason for his recycling. He had a dishevelled appearance and his demeanour was not high-military spit and polish. Near the end of basic training, on some relaxed time on a Sunday, he invited me to go upstairs in the barracks and smoke a joint.

"What, here? Are you fuckin' crazy?" I asked.

"Yeah, I'm crazy," he said, "but come on up, it's all right, there's no lifers around."

I thought what the hell, what are they gonna do, put me in the Army and send me to Vietnam? Truth be known, I had smoked marijuana on numerous occasions in my civilian life. I had even bought a few lids. I wasn't an habitual pothead, but I occasionally liked to get high with friends and thought there was nothing wrong with it, other than it being illegal.

We went upstairs and I saw a small gathering of guys huddled in the far corner. I joined the clusterfuck and soon the joints were being passed around and we were all giggling, chukin' and jivin' and having a splendid time. My new friend reached into his pants and pulled out a small bottle. He took a pull, wiped his mouth with the back of his hand, and, just like in the movies, went AAARRGH! I noticed the bottle had a Robitussin label on it, but I assumed it was smuggled booze camouflaged in a cough syrup bottle. It turned out that it was indeed Robitussin. He loved the stuff because it had codeine. He offered it all around; no one accepted. He shrugged and took another swig.

Among the group, I was surprised to see the trainee platoon sergeant, a nice guy who had re-enlisted. He had been in the Army before, gotten discharged, and then had been a civilian so long that he had to start all over again in Basic with us. He intended to be a career soldier and he would go on to every specialty school he could get into. He eventually became an Airborne Ranger Special Forces Medic. His thinking may have been that if the Army spent big bucks to train and educate him, then perhaps they would be reluctant to waste his life thoughtlessly. There appeared to be no shortage of cash or lives spent, however, as the KIA numbers were high at this time, averaging a couple hundred per week.

On one particularly long and gruelling run back to the company area from the beach ranges where we trained with M-14 weapons, I had my first verbal altercation with an officer of the United States Army. I could usually keep pace with the best of them, but today I was lagging behind with the slower section of the main pack. In front of us were the guys who could run like gazelles, and do it all day long. A lieutenant spotted me, all red in the face, and made a cheap shot. Some verbal sparring occurred between us, which he interpreted as a puke questioning his authority. He bird-dogged me the remaining two miles back to the company street. "Brown, pick up your pace, in combat you'll be left behind to die alone." I thought that I was running hard enough; besides, he carried no gear. We were humping weapons, steel pots, web gear, and ponchos. Just as I crossed the finish line, another officer held out his arm in front of me and created two groups: the faster gazelles who got to go to the PX for a beer bust, and the slower boots like me who got sent to the barracks to sort themselves out. Instead of being resentful, I saw it as a golden opportunity to get back to the barracks, smoke as many butts as possible, and stand by for the next mind-fuck. Running was never my area of expertise anyway.

As trainees, we were constantly being introduced to new toys, and trained in their use. We learned to neatly arrange, clean, polish, display, and hang from our bodies things like helmet liners, web gear, ammo pouches, ponchos, first-aid kits, and what have you. Each day's training block required specific dress-up instructions so we would all look the same. Being boy soldiers, we were quick to catch on to all the new gadgets and the infinite combinations of display. The DIs would bark, "Let's get it on," and we immediately put on all our equipment as told. In Vietnam, where we would be told to "Saddle up," we would hang our toys from our bodies according to our own personal preferences.

The hand grenade phase of training was intimidating. We had all heard the story of a recent recruit who had muffed his grenade and had blown himself and his instructor up. The carnage had been limited to the two of them thanks to the thick concrete walls that separated the grenade-throwing sites. One recruit, one instructor, one grenade – you had to hand it to the Army, they had it wired for sound. When most people think of grenades, they think of the Audie Murphy type, with the bumps all over them, but the grenades we used were shaped like baseballs. I guess some ingenious American must have said, "Hey, let's shape it like a baseball – every American kid can throw a baseball." Everything we learned about throwing grenades was by the numbers:

assume position, pull pin, throw grenade, and recover. We practised the drill repeatedly. Later as grunts in Vietnam, we would play with them like young boys playing with firecrackers. When the spindle flew off as the grenade was released from the thrower's hand, there was a four- to seven-second delay before detonation. In Vietnam, we'd add a step to the drill. We would pull the pin, pop the spindle, delay as long as we dared, and then throw the grenade.

While I was in basic training being prepared for battle, the U.S. continued its strategy of large-scale search and destroy missions. Thirty thousand American soldiers had already died by the time Richard Nixon had taken office. Another ten thousand would die his first year as president. Rumours about the carnage of Hamburger Hill ran rampant through boot camp. I tried to get a mental picture of what that must have been like, but found it difficult to visualize. In Vietnam, I would learn more about Hamburger Hill from some of the survivors. Troopers of the famous 101st Airborne Division had been inserted into the A Shau Valley and had taken ludicrous casualties to capture Apbia Mountain. The survivors described the mountain as a series of ridges heavily fortified by the enemy. Fighting uphill against guys who were well dug-in while your ass was exposed didn't sound like good strategy to me.

* * *

Graduation was just around the corner. We maggots were feeling fit in our new bodies, and anxious to get on with it. With perfect timing, sensing our elation, the U.S. Army released the military occupation specialty list. The moment is flash frozen in my mind. I found my name easily: Brown, Leslie D., US 56741366, 11B. Eleven Bravo: I was to be a light weapons infantryman. I was stunned. I had given my all, played the game, and this was my reward.

There followed a flurry of activity, probably intended to distract our attention for now. All those who had combat MOSs were herded onto trucks and sent to the beach ranges for a one-day crash course on the M-16, the Army's answer to the communist AK-47. Our mood changed as we absorbed the news about our new jobs. We automatically began to distance ourselves from the lucky ones with non-combat MOSs. We Eleven Bravos formed an even smaller sub-group from among those with combat specialties; we further distanced ourselves from the others. The Army's newest were a silent minority.

Graduation was held on the huge parade field adjacent to our company area. We demonstrated our new marching skills in front of loved ones who lived close enough to the Monterey Peninsula to make the trek to Fort Ord. They watched their boy soldiers receive praise from those who had just yesterday called them maggots. My mom, dad, and younger sister Virginia were there, as was Nancy, who had driven up with my family. The crowd was large, and very, very quiet. They were the silent majority.

We got the weekend off after graduation. We would report Monday morning to our Advanced Individual Training Company located conveniently just down the street. My folks and sister would drive back to L.A. that night; Nancy stayed with me for the weekend. My dad had rented us a room in a local no-tell motel and had even thrown in a bottle of syrupy sweet Mogen David wine. As my mother was leaving, I could see that the stress of another son in the military was already taking its toll. In many ways, my tour would be tougher on her than it would be on me.

3. AIT

Fellow trainees in front of the barracks, Fort Ord.

was amazed at how quickly we were settled into our new barracks as the Advanced Individual Training began. We knew the drill and could have trained ourselves had somebody left strategically placed notes around, with the numbers clearly legible. There was an absence of drill instructors too; instead of one DI per platoon, they had streamlined to one master drill sergeant for the entire company. He had help from non-DI corporals who wanted to be DIs when they grew up.

At the time, we never considered the plight of those who had to carry out the nasty business of preparing us for war. We were busy dealing with our own troubles. I'm sure now that many of those who helped to churn out the endless stream of grunts secretly had reservations about the war, but after a twenty-year career as a professional grunt, what were they going to do, quit and become brain surgeons? Most were Vietnam vets and wore the Combat Infantryman Badge (CIB) which meant they had seen and survived combat. We were junior grunts and were inferior because we had no cool splashes of colour on our now rapidly fading olive drab fatigues.

Soon after we had arrived in AIT, we were each required to individually meet our new Company Commander. I suspect the meeting of each grunt was the Army's way of proving that they were progressive, and had a liberal, "open-door" policy. Our new commander was actually a first lieutenant. They must have been short of captains, due to the green machine needing them in Vietnam. Our commander appeared to us to be a very unhappy human being.

I had planned to discuss with him my status as a Canadian citizen in the U.S. army, and how it didn't seem fair to be a grunt. I knocked on his door and was told to enter. I figured I'd put the unhappy lieutenant at ease right away so we could have meaningful dialogue about my situation. I smiled as I saluted, and said "Private Brown reports as ordered, sir."

I, of course, had added an extra step to the by-the-numbers drill by smiling. Naturally this was unacceptable to the lieutenant who knew an extra number when he saw one.

"Don't smile at me, you fuckin' faggot!" he exploded. "Now get outside and try that again."

I entered again, this time by the numbers, and was ordered to stand ill at ease.

"Brown, are you a fuckin' faggot?"

"No, sir."

"Any problems?"

"No, sir."

"Any questions?"

"No, sir."

"Dismissed. Next."

I shouldn't be too hard on the lieutenant. He had 160 welcome-to-the-unit speeches to give, and he was only on the Bs.

I had been in the United States Army for ten weeks now and I had not found one single thing to laugh about. I missed laughing, and hoped to do it again some day. Sure, I had smiled, like the time we smoked joints back in Basic, but good old lighthearted belly-laughing was gone and wouldn't return for a very long time.

In AIT, we became intimate with our new toy, the M-16 assault rifle. The sixteen was nothing like the M-14 we had our last love affair with. "This is my weapon [hold up rifle]. This is my gun [grab crotch]. This is for fightin' [hold up rifle]. This is for fun [grab crotch]." We had already been taught in Basic that dropping your weapon was worse than cheating on your wife as it was a much more deserving object of your affections, "cause it could save your life in combat, you stupid fuckers." Now, we were taught to love our sixteens and were encouraged to take them to bed and hold them gently in our arms and promise them that we would never forsake them for another.

We fired shit-loads of ammunition in AIT. In Basic, we had received training in all aspects of military life, ranging from the universal code of military justice to how to extract your bayonet from a dead guy. AIT was different; now we were light weapons specialists. We carried the M-16 and fired it almost daily. The focus in basic training had been conventional battle training. The focus in AIT was switched to jungle warfare training.

We now had new names for the enemy, too. He was to be known as gook, dink, slope, Vietcong, Charlie, and little yellow commie fucker. Some at first were justifiably reluctant to use these new names for the enemy, but that reluctance would be short-lived.

The Army had been in the grunt-training business for a very long time when we got to AIT. They had a myriad of villages and jungle trails and assault courses all set up for us to play in. The trails were very well worn by our predecessor grunt trainees. On one particular exercise, the instructors told us to move out down this make-believe Vietcong trail and stay alert. One astute grunt asked, "But, Sarge, I thought you told us to never use the trails."

"Shut up, puke, and stick to the program," the Sarge replied. So we all duly ditty-bopped down the trail. Some of us died by sniper fire from the trees, some from simulated booby traps, and some from a dink ambush. We all pretend died and the Sarge repeated the key words "stay alert." Many of the courses were live fire. We would get on line moving forward, firing our sixteens, and quickly learned how not to shoot each other in the back.

The M-16 was all black, shorter than you might expect, with no wooden parts. It had a selector switch on the left side of the weapon; the positions were safe, semi, and auto. With the flick of your thumb, you could select the mode of preference and fire. If the sixteen was in the auto position, and the trigger was just barely touched, it would fire a two- to three-round burst. It was a rapid-firing weapon, and on full automatic, the barrel would rise up and drift to the right. There was very little recoil, and a weird springy noise emitted from the hard plastic stock. In AIT, they worked well. Mine never jammed, as it was well cleaned and oiled daily. In Vietnam, where conditions were much less ideal, it would jam sometimes. The things fired just too damned fast. With its wooden stock, the tried-and-true M-14 was the one I preferred.

We were trained in the use of many different weapons: the M-60 belt-fed machine gun; the M-79 grenade launcher; the .45 pistol; the shoulder-fired light anti-tank weapon (LAW); the big guy of machine guns, the .50-calibre; the devastating claymore anti-personnel mine; hand grenades; white phosphorus grenades; and CS gas canisters. We learned how to call in artillery and mortar fire, and adjust the fire on target. We were taught first aid, map reading, compass and orienteering, escape and evasion, radio operations, and how to guide in a helicopter. The only thing they could not give us was experience, but we'd pick that up later.

The mind-fucks and psychological abuse were starting to take their toll, and guys were losin' it. In my platoon barracks one night at four in the morning, a fight between grunts erupted. One grunt chased another with an entrenching tool, vowing to cut his head off. None of us other grunts wanted to get too close, but eventually we got together and subdued the combatants. Another guy, from Colorado, got drunk one weekend and was en route to "kick some lifer ass," then desert and hide out in the Rockies with his dogs. I was closest to him at the time, and attempted to talk him out of it. He was not in a talkative mood, and, as one might guess, turned on me. We ended up in a huggy, teary heap on the floor, as he eventually chilled. Guys were pacing in the barracks late at night, and moaning and groaning in their sleep. I myself was stressed out and had no idea what to expect next. I was close to desertion, but couldn't make myself take that step.

I felt a growing sense of shame about being in the Army. On weekends, when we got a pass to go "dip our wicks," I would fly to L.A. to be with my family and Nancy. As a member of the military, I could fly standby and get a better rate, but I had to wear my Class A dress uniform to get the friendly deal. Not wanting to be identified in public as an infantryman, I would wear my 501s and a tee shirt instead. The cost to fly from Monterey to Burbank Airport was equivalent to one month's pay for me, so my mom would quietly subsidize some of my weekend trips.

* * *

In AIT, we were constantly told that the U.S. would win in Vietnam by using good old American devastating superior firepower. For every bullet that the enemy would fire at us, we would fire millions back. Unbeknownst to many on either side of the border, Canadian factories produced and provided a substantial quantity of the ammunition used in the war. As the cash flowed north, most Canadians had no reason to be suspicious. Though Canadians sincerely believed Canada was neutral, many were quietly profiting from the war.

All the while, young Canadian men continued to trickle over the border to enlist. National and international laws were being broken, but both governments looked the other way. I suspect Canada didn't want to draw media attention to the issue and the U.S. could certainly use the bodies to feed the green machine.

Canadians came for all kinds of different reasons. Some came for adventure, to get away from the old man or a small town with limited opportunities. Some came to test themselves, to see how they'd react in war. Some came because they sincerely believed in what the U.S. was doing in Vietnam in trying to stop the spread of communism. I can't fathom the culture shock these young Canadians must have faced. At least I had twelve years to get used to the American way.

* * *

We were fully trained grunts, lacking only in experience, when we received our orders. Naturally, we would all be going to Vietnam, nicknamed Paradise. I was to report to Fort Lewis, Washington, 5 Oct 69 for shipment.

4. RANGER BATTALION

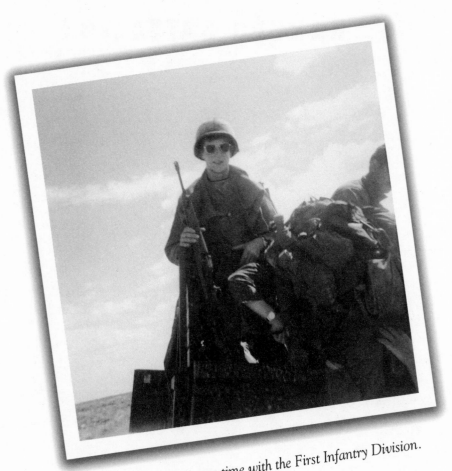

On a truck, during my time with the First Infantry Division.

fter AIT, the U.S. Army generously gave the new grunts two weeks' leave. I didi maued back to L.A. to spend what little time I had left with my family and Nancy. I was relieved to be out of training but found it impossible not to think about my rapidly approaching one-year tour of duty. I partied and played, but my mood would swing rapidly. I noticed that some friends had difficulty saying goodbye; many were unable to make eye contact. I found a storage lot to park my '47 Chev Woody. I hated the thought of abandoning my trusty surf mobile. It, like me, was not going to the beach any time soon.

Nancy and my mother were beyond being emotional, and would spontaneously erupt into tears in my presence. I tried to reassure them that President Nixon had a new plan and that the war would end soon. Privately, I had no idea what to expect. Nixon had vowed to not be the first President to lose a war. He was, after all, a Republican and a communist-hater.

A few friends had recently returned from Vietnam, and I pumped them for information. Ron had enlisted in the Marine Corps right out of high school. He sported two full-forearm, multi-coloured, snake-and-dagger "Death Before Dishonor" USMC tattoos. He had been a door gunner in Vietnam and was currently serving as a brig guard at Camp Pendleton. The jail guard gig sounded horrendous. He described the psycho inmates and their fully guaranteed regular beatings. After thirteen months of trying to kill Vietnamese people, he now had to abuse his own. I thought again about my good fortune in evading the Marine sergeant at the induction centre who had volunteered the draftees for the crotch. I now told that story to Ron who said, "Those guys are fucked, they'll be harassed to death." Ron tried to be supportive and reassuring. He said, "Don't worry about it, you're in the Army. Everybody knows the real fightin' is done by Marines." He spoke little of his Vietnam experience, but his silence was deafening.

Another friend, Bob, had gone the crotch route as well and had just returned from Paradise the month prior. I had never seen Bob smoke up before his tour, but when we got together one night after his return, he was rollin' up the doobies at a furious rate. He had smuggled the pot home from Vietnam. I was amazed at its potency and was unable to keep up with him.

Bob had seen heavy combat up around Hue while he had served in a tank unit. He spoke of beaucoup dead gooks, and how some guys would cut off the testicles of a dead enemy and stick them back in the mouth of the corpse. Bob's advice was very clear: "Don't go. Run and don't look back." Even at this late date, I still thought of deserting, but in my state of denial, I continued to hope the Army would come to its senses and place me in a non-combat job.

My family had asked Ron to drive me to L.A. International Airport, as they were unable to take me themselves. He came to pick me up at 5:00 a.m. My mother, Nancy, and I had said our goodbyes the night before. My dad, though, met me in the darkened hallway that morning. Not a word was spoken between us. We held each other and cried, then I was gone. Years later, both my mother and Nancy would tell me that they thought they'd never see me alive again.

* * *

I hated wearing that Class A uniform with its Crossed Rifles and Blue Infantry Rope. This was a civilian flight, of course, and I was relieved to see that nobody paid any attention to me, probably because I didn't as yet have any cool patches and ribbons that would denote me as a baby-killer. As I recall, it was a direct flight to the Seattle/Tacoma airport, where the Army had buses ready to deliver us to Fort Lewis, Washington. There, we were quickly in-processed. Some more poking, prodding, and corralling was done. We all carried shot records on our person so we could show them when ordered. Those who still needed some shots were shot up on the spot to make sure we didn't catch God knows what diseases. I have no idea how many shots we got, but the Army had been injecting us with all kinds of stuff since day one in basic training. I guess needles were expensive because they had these really cool air guns that just blasted the stuff into our skin. We could simply walk station to station, get blasted, and move on for more. The airgun blaster operators would say, "Let your arm go limp, stupid, and it won't hurt so much."

We also turned in our Class A uniforms. Apparently, we didn't need them any more. We went in one end of a huge warehouse in Class As and out the other end in olive drab jungle fatigues complete with our names on them. I noticed guys coming out of another exit all decked out in Class As with cool splashes of colour all over them. The new grunts recognized them straight away. They were the old grunts and didn't look like us

at all. I guessed that the food in Vietnam was unappe-
tizing cause the old grunts were kind of gaunt-looking
and the heat and sun must have been hard on the eyes
because they looked damaged.

Adjacent to the World War II barracks, where we
were guests, there was this really quaint white cottage
complete with white picket fence and manicured lawn.
We walked by and noticed the sign hanging at the
entrance. It informed the reader that supper hours were
1700–1900 hours. The menu was steak grilled to order
and was for returning Vietnam personnel only. Some of
us got KP duty in the quaint cottage and had to serve the
congratulatory steak dinner to the returnees. My karma
was good that day, because I didn't get KP duty. Those
that did, didn't talk about it. We all cackled like old hens
at the absurdity of it all: Survive the war, get a steak
dinner; get your shit blown away, and your mom gets a
check for $10,000.

At Fort Lewis, I hung out with Cotter, Benton, and
Dunne. We had gone through Basic and AIT together
and had a lot in common. We were all from suburb com-
munities around L.A., and we were all junior college
dropout draftees. I, of course, was the only Canadian.
My brother, Ken, who had by now served two tours in
Vietnam as a sailor, was home, so I figured I'd be the
new token Canadian in Vietnam. Decades later, when
meeting Canadian Vietnam vets, we would tell each

other the same thing: "I thought I was the only one."

After four days at Fort Lewis, the Army bused us to McChord Air Force Base, conveniently located nearby. Our flight path would include stops in Hawaii and Guam. Air carriers must have fought ferociously for the lucrative contracts to safely deliver us in modern jumbo jets to our ultimate destination. I forget the name of the carrier but think it was a foreign outfit. The stewardesses were young, smiley, blonde, beautiful, and they kept their distance. They served us hot dogs, potato chips, and Cokes – all-American food for the boys. The smoking lamp was always lit; those that had 'em smoked 'em and by the time we landed in Honolulu our ashtrays runneth over. While we explored Honolulu International Airport, they emptied them out, obviously the true reason for our touchdown. They must have been expecting trouble because everywhere we looked, we saw hordes of military policemen and the oversized goons of the shore patrol – all were armed. We tended to huddle together in the terminal, dressed in too-dark green jungle fatigues and jungle boots with the annoying anti-punji-stick plate in the sole. After about 20,000 klicks, the boots actually got broken in and probably felt to us much like the finely crafted moccasins of North American Aboriginal warriors must have felt to them as they went off to war.

In Guam, we were emphatically ordered not to exit the military terminal, as swift punishment would surely follow. We all milled around for hours amongst the Guamanians and mostly Air Force personnel. The Air Force had lots of their big expensive flying toys coming and going. Many were B-52s. The departing ones, laden with huge bombs tucked up out of sight in their bellies, lumbered around showing signs of their burdensome weight.

Soon enough, we were airborne again. More junk food for the boys, more attempts at much-needed slumber, and more smokin'. Some wondered out loud, when would we get our sixteens? Would we have the opportunity to zero our weapons – adjust the sights – before hitting the trenches and killing commies for our mommies? At this late date in the war, shouldn't it be expected that they would have sorted this thing out by now, and let us cherry grunts know what was going down? Just prior to final approach, the captain of the craft joked that the weather was, of course, unbearably hot and enemy incoming rocket and mortar fire was light to moderate.

There were no trenches nor was there any incoming. There were more buses, however, and they had screens on the windows to prevent explosive devices from being thrown at us by the enemy, whoever and wherever he was. We learned that we were now at the repo-depot, the Ninetieth Replacement Battalion at Cam Ranh Bay. Apparently, there were world-class white-sand beaches there, but we did not get the opportunity to frolic on them. One night, two nights there, and we had our orders.

Dunne and I were assigned to the famed First Infantry Division. The next day we would start travelling to join our unit. Cotter and Benton were going up to the Americal Division, ill famed because of its involvement in the Mylai massacre incident, which had occurred the year before and which, when the story got out, would shock the world. Cotter, Benton, Dunne, and I had landed on the soil of the Republic of Vietnam on 9 Oct 69. With lots of luck our date of eligible return from overseas, known as our DEROS, would be 8 Oct 70.

There were truck rides, a plane ride I think, perhaps more trucks, and eventually Dunne and I were deposited at the First Infantry Division spot for FNGs. FNGs stood for fuckin' new guys, which is what everyone called us. (The Army could not, of course, refer to us as fuckin' new guys. They insisted we were *funny* new guys.) The FNGs were fed and housed for one night at that location. We were further in-processed the next day, then off by truck towards Di An, just north of Saigon, for, of all things, in-country training. As a fuckin' new guy, I was busy absorbing the sights, sounds, and smells of my new surroundings. It was, indeed, a different kind of place.

On the truck ride to Di An, we met a mid-tour grunt in transit back to his unit from R&R. His boots were unpolished and his demeanour was guarded. It was a lengthy truck ride of several hours so eventually he started pointing things out to us. "There's LBJ," he said nonchalantly, not referring to Lyndon Baines Johnson but Long Binh Jail, where the malingerers and law-breaker grunts were housed and tortured. To me the warehouse building, located in a fenced-in compound, resembled a large black steel oven. Dunne and I glanced at each other, and we both made a face.

At some point, we saw a huge white statue prominently located adjacent to the four-lane highway. Our grunt guide said, "Oh, that's the statue honouring soldiers of the worthless South Vietnamese Army." We knew our politics: the Army of the Republic of Vietnam, or ARVN, was our ally. We also saw a huge sprawling white complex that was the major headquarters of some agency or other. The highway that led to it, Highway 1, was damned near gridlocked as military and civilian vehicles competed to get there first. There was all kinds of noise, lights, pollution, and congestion. Eventually, we got dropped off right where we needed to be, at the First Division's in-country training camp. We thought: "Hey cool, five more days of M-16 rifle shootin', hand grenade throwin' and claymore blowin' practice, plus the added bonus of being five days closer to our DEROS."

We grunts had a lesson to learn right off the bat: grunts were in the minority. Most of the guys reporting for in-country training were non-grunts, and had yet to touch an M-16 rifle. Over the years, I've heard many different figures given for the ratio of infantrymen to support personnel. I tend to believe the twelve or fifteen to one figure, myself. This meant that for every light weapons specialist fielded in Vietnam, there were twelve to fifteen support people to supply him with food, drink, ammo, intelligence, medical treatment, and transportation. Whatever the true figures were, it was undeniable that grunts were spread more thinly than one might guess.

Dunne, myself, and some other grunt replacements were hangin' in a six-man clusterfuck drinking Cokes after training when we were approached by an officer – I think he was a major. He strode up to us in a cocky way and said, "Hey, lookey here, some fuckin' new guys." Being FNGs, we had no response. Even though we were green as green gets, we instinctively knew by his highly polished jungle boots, his freshly starched tailored jungle fatigues, and his lack of a Combat Infantryman Badge that he was a non-grunt. He apparently sensed what we were thinking, because his demeanour softened as he asked where we were from and what our MOS was. We all responded with our hometowns and Eleven-Bravo, not once throwing in a "sir." He eventually left our clusterfuck alone and we all thought, "Boy, good thing we're not REMFs (rear echelon mother fuckers) or he would have really fucked with us."

As the in-country training progressed, it became obvious it was geared to REMFs and personnel that had never fired an M-16. They did have one demonstration, though, that we all paid very close attention to. That was the sapper demonstration. They even had a real live Vietnamese sapper on hand to prove to us that they could sneak up on us in the dark and extinguish our young green lives in fifty-seven different ways. I thought to myself, "Okay, now there he is. I'm looking at my first enemy soldier." The sapper, dressed in a loin cloth and bandanna, had oiled flesh and leered at us as he slithered and snaked in and around numerous layers of concertina wire rigged with trip flares, and then exited without causing any bleeding or tripping any flares. An appreciation for his resolve, resourcefulness, and killing skills was taking root.

Near the end of our in-country training, we all went out on a patrol "outside the wire" with an instructor. He said, "Stay alert. These training patrols have made contact with the enemy in the past." We ran a textbook-style patrol using a main column flanked on both sides by other columns. We made no contact that day, and I never again saw grunts operate a patrol that way in actual jungle areas.

Dunne and I were on the buddy system, without signin' up for it. We were both assigned to Bravo Company Second Battalion Sixteenth Infantry, also known as the Ranger Battalion. It had recently departed the Di An vicinity and now had its basecamp at Lai Khe, a town clustered in and around a Michelin rubber plantation a couple of hours by truck away. En route, we noticed that the terrain was flat and that the area was quite populated. We saw numerous schools, pharmacies, houses, buildings large and small, and lots of Vietnamese people, who rarely looked our way. As we approached the basecamp, I knew we were much closer to the war. There were towers and wire and members of the popular force armed with M-1 carbines guarding the gate. The PFs were sort of a civilian militia. Most wore black silky garments resembling pyjamas, straw conical hats, and what we all called Ho Chi Minh sandals, a recycled tire affair, with straps of whatever material was available.

With the village at the centre, an airstrip, and all the military personnel there from various battalions, Lai Khe was a major basecamp. We were dumped off inside where we reported as ordered at battalion headquarters. We then walked to our company area, which consisted of an orderly room, a supply room, and other small cottage-sized buildings. Dunne and I were greeted by the company clerk in the orderly room, which was sort of the company business office. We were officially documented on paper and told to go over to Supply. We got to Supply and were again greeted by the company clerk. "The supply sergeant got blown away about a week ago," the clerk explained. "A black grunt came in from the field and ordered up some clean fatigues. The supply sergeant refused so the grunt flipped his selector to auto and put a five-round burst in ol' Sarge's chest. He died right here where I'm standin'." Later, in the field, this story was corroborated by grunts who had nothing to gain by misleading us. We turned in our four remaining sets of new state-of-the-art jungle fatigues with our names on them. "You'll get clean fatigues when they are available," the clerk said. It was a socialized laundry system. We grunts shared communal clothes, but only got clean ones when the Army gave them to us. Dunne and I got all the grunt stuff, including our M-16s.

We had bunker guard that night and were to go to Firebase Lorraine, which had been named after the battalion commander's wife, the following morning on the daily convoy. Bunker guard involved a dusk-to-dawn occupation of a fighting position on the bunker line securing the basecamp. The fighting position was a rectangular hole in the ground large enough for three. Three of us alternated guard, and slept on the ground around the hole. That's where I got bit by an Asian spider or some such critter. By morning, my upper lip was swollen to the size of a mini pork roast and I was forced to seek medical attention. The medics gave me some pills and said, "Stay here one more night and catch the convoy tomorrow." Dunne departed that day, I the next, for Firebase Lorraine.

The convoy I left with on the next day consisted of several trucks with supplies. Some pulled potable-water tanks, others Howitzers. We left the basecamp around ten. The trip took hours since the trucks crawled along as fast as the mortar platoon could walk, sweeping the road for mines. I was armed but ammo-less. Another occupant on our truck flipped me a fully loaded magazine and said, "Insert the magazine but don't chamber a round."

Finally, we arrived at the smallish firebase. There was a flurry of activity as troops dismounted and supplies were delivered. The firebase was a circular affair approximately one-and-a-half football fields in diameter. There were no buildings but lots of bunkers were scattered throughout amongst the numerous artillery pieces and mortar tubes. The big guns, the 155mm Howitzers, and heavy mortar tubes were here to provide us grunts with superior American firepower twenty-four hours a day. I was directed to Bravo Company's area where I met up with Dunne. He was grinning like an old salt, having had one more day in the field than me.

I met my squad leader who took me over to a huge heap of ordnance. He rummaged through the pile and started throwing ammo and things in my direction. "There, that's a basic load," he said. "Now pack that shit in your ruck along with enough c-rations and water for a three- to five-day operation." To organize and pack up all the fightin' stuff was no small task and I spent the afternoon sorting and arranging, trying various methods in an effort to hang all the stuff from my body. The basic load included 400 rounds M-16 ammo, 100 rounds M-60 machine gun ammo, 4 baseball-type fragmentation grenades, 1 light anti-tank weapon (LAW), 1 claymore mine and bag, 2 smoke grenades of assorted colour and

1 large bar of c-4 explosive. I had seen all of these weapons of destruction before; all were familiar to me. What was new was having so much and all together in a heap at my feet. I thought that I should perhaps refrain from smoking, but quickly got over that as the next nic craving materialized. I filled my canteens (8 quarts) with potable water from the trailers, arranged loaded magazines in bandoleers, hooked things here and there and thought I'd stand up for a test spin around the perimeter. I had all the fightin' gear on when I made my first attempts to get up. I couldn't manage it because the fulcrum and weight distributions were askew. I then tried rolling sideways from the overturned turtle position and found that I could get onto all fours but was stuck there. Miraculously, I got one knee up. Then using my sixteen as a friend, I eventually gained a standing position. If I leaned forward, the momentum of the weight would take over and I'd have to walk faster to compensate. If I leaned back, I'd instantly fall backwards. It would take weeks to finetune the gear, and that would happen on the move, as we were to make an air combat assault the next day.

I was feeling exhausted. I had not a real night's sleep since I left California one and a half weeks ago. I was operating on youthful juices that, with time in-country, would prove not to be without limits. There was lots going on in my head, but mostly it was fear. I was scared shitless, literally. I had not had a decent bowel movement in much too long a time. It would be many days before I could resolve my personal problem.

Late afternoon, we got ordered to run a RIF (recon in force) beyond the wire to make sure there weren't any bad guys poised there to stage a night attack. It was a squad-sized group of seven guys. Other squads were also out looking for the enemy. The Captain of Bravo Company was set up with his command group about one and a half klicks outside the wire. His position was secured by another platoon of Bravo and we all sort of linked up there for a powwow with the Captain. It was hot, damned hot, so hot I thought I'd pass out, and we were only carrying our fightin' gear, no rucksacks. The captain, for the benefit of Dunne and me, gave us a quick physical description of our flat area of operations (AO) and what we were up against. Apparently, there were beaucoup Vietcong and NVA soldiers operating in the area. All four companies plus the recon platoon were operating in the AO and were regularly making contact. The VC tended to move in small groups but maintained large bunker complexes throughout the AO. The enemy was frequently rocketing Lai Khe from our AO and was scoring good hits. Booby traps were abundant, and larger groups of VC would ambush and engage squads, platoons, and companies. The good news, according to the Captain, was that the enemy was hungry. "If we can't kill 'im with weapons, we'll starve him to death." He went on to explain quickly a plan by Command to deprive the enemy of rice by clamping down on the local villagers who had in the past helped the Vietcong. Our platoon moved out of the impromptu classroom and was replaced by another platoon, which presumably got the same spiel. We provided security for that powwow.

I was placed with Johnson, a black grunt from Washington, D.C. His first name was Marcel so naturally everybody called him Frenchy. Frenchy was field-stripping cigarettes big time. He'd empty all the tobacco from them and fill them back up with a green-brown leafy substance resembling marijuana. Frenchy would occasionally look my way and smile.

"What's your name and where you from?" he eventually asked.

"Brown and Los Angeles," I answered. There was little you could do with my name, so everybody called me Brown.

"You smoke dew, Brown?"

"Maybe, but what the heck is dew?" I said.

Frenchy laughed. "It's pot, man, and you got lots to learn. Tonight, after dark, we'll smoke these."

Frenchy was right, I did have lots to learn, starting with the language. Like GI jungle culture itself, the lingo was constantly evolving. It was a mixture of English, French, Vietnamese, and military jargon, both proper and slang. I'd be fluent soon enough and could then speak with the culturally correct tongue of a grunt. Infantrymen didn't walk, they humped; they didn't eat, they chowed down; they didn't sleep, they caught Zs; they didn't die, they bought the farm, got wasted, greased, zapped, met their maker, or got their shit blown away.

So, we humped back to the firebase, chowed down, smoked dew, set out our claymores, and tried to catch some Zs. As perimeter security, we rotated guard duty, dusk to dawn, with one man awake and alert at each of the many bunker fighting positions. Outgoing artillery rounds and mortar fire were constant on a firebase, sometimes rising in tempo, sometimes falling, but never ceasing, day or night. The cannon cockers had a wide range of projectiles to choose from: there was the standard high explosive (HE), the flare, the fleshette, the white phosphorus, the gas, the delayed fuse, the treetop proximity fuse air bursts, and many more. Naturally, 100 per cent detonation of these rounds was impossible so the AO was littered with zillions of dud rounds. Air strikes also left behind dud bombs of small and large varieties, any of which could explode any time, for no other reason than that they could.

* * *

My first helicopter insertion in Vietnam is one I remember in detail. I had noticed that the mood of the platoon had been jovial, almost happy, on the firebase. Now, that mood was replaced with a quiet seriousness as we saddled up and prepared for our combat assault. We were to be inserted into an artillery-prepped landing zone (LZ), a clearing in the jungle large enough to accommodate the four slicks that would carry our platoon.

We assembled on the "pad" in prearranged clusters of grunts and boarded the slicks. Once airborne, the slicks grouped into a classic diamond-formation, with a lead slick, a tail slick, and flanking slicks. I was in the slick on the left flank, situated against the wall in the centre. The open doorways were reserved for the vet grunts who liked to dangle their feet and get a good look around. I was somewhere between terrified and hysterical, and was searching my memory about what to do upon landing. I noticed two more helicopters had joined the gaggle of slicks, one on each flank. They were gunships, sporting rocket pods and mini-guns. The gunship flew so close on our flank that it looked as if I could reach out and touch it. It must be a hot LZ, I thought, if we got us a gunship escort.

As the gaggle descended, I could see the approaching landing zone. I was startled as both gunships went to work. I watched the long white projectiles leave their pods and could see their vapour trail until the rockets exploded in the tree line. It was a blending of the B-R-R-R-P of mini-guns and the sound of launched rockets. This bombardment continued until we almost touched down, and then the gunships skyed up. The door gunners now went to work with their M-60 machines guns, directing their fire into the tree line. I watched red tracers disappear into a brownish red dust cloud kicked up by the striking rounds. The ships flared, hovering just above the ground, and touched down simultaneously. The door gunners ceased fire so as not to shoot the grunts as we unassed the ships. Some grunts had leapt off the slicks prior to touchdown forcing the pilots to scramble for control of their crafts. This premature unassing of slicks, with its sudden and erratic weight loss, was a practice slick crews disliked. Grunts, on the other hand, were understandably anxious to get away from a slow-moving flying target. Air crews, too, it must be said, were anxious to get off the ground and away from fire. Our slicks clattered off. The silence that followed was severe.

We hunched over, leaning forward with our knees bent to make a shorter target. Some grunts fired into the tree line, but we all moved forward to our respective positions, hoping to enhance our life expectancy by being aggressive. Once we reached our positions, we instinctively proned-out with our faces as deep in the ground as possible, and awaited return fire. This face-down position, with an eighty-pound rucksack on our backs, was one we assumed often. Time in this position was suspended; we would drift in our own individual thoughts, awaiting whatever was to come.

As no return fire was detected, the point element formed up and moved away from the LZ on a prearranged azimuth. The other riflemen, RTOs, thump gunners, machine gun teams, and the platoon leader's group fell into their order of march for that day. We did not bunch up, keeping good interval so one round would not get us all. The action of forming up and moving out was accomplished in an orderly fashion as the platoon transformed itself into a single snake-like column.

At first, the jungle vegetation was thin, and Williams, the pointman, did not have to use a machete to get through. Not too far from the LZ, maybe one klick, Williams dropped and assumed the proned-out position. The entire platoon instantly did the same. Williams had seen movement in front. The squad leader removed his ruck and low-crawled up alongside Williams to see what was happening. Williams whispered that he had seen two armed VC run into a clump of thick vegetation. The squad leader whispered into his RTO's handset and reported what had happened. The lieutenant whispered back, ordering the point squad to form a skirmish line and conduct a recon by fire. Recon by fire meant we would shoot the heck out of that clump of bushes and then move forward to see what we got. I was in the point squad so I, along with the rest of the squad and one machine gun team, quietly removed my ruck while still prone and low-crawled up on line. The rest of the platoon circled the wagons to form a defensive perimeter.

With good interval between grunts, on line, we opened fire. The noise was deafening as M-16s, one thump gun, and one machine gun delivered their projectiles into the bush. Soon, someone commanded us to cease fire. Complete silence followed. The smoke from spent cartridges lingered in the jungle heat and we waited. After a few moments, we rose up and moved forward on line towards the bush. Any former occupants were gone but we did find a trail of blood. The lieutenant ordered the other rifle squad, along with the other machine gun team, to follow the blood trail. My squad linked up with the rest of the platoon. We moved approximately 100 metres, and again formed a circular defensive perimeter. The squad that had followed the blood trail radioed back, reporting that the trail had dissipated. They returned and re-enforced the defensive perimeter. Every enemy soldier in the AO now knew where we were and how many of us there were. In fact, the enemy usually knew more about how grunts operated than we did.

The platoon again formed up into a snake-line column. Dusk was rapidly approaching and to stay there was to invite the enemy to engage. We moved slowly and cautiously with the knowledge that he was out there. The vegetation thickened and Williams had to hack his way through. Spent, he called for a replacement. I made my short-lived pointman debut, learned nothing but more fear. I resumed my new-guy stumbling behind the squad's radio telephone operator.

Dusk was upon us as the platoon sergeant and lieutenant discussed where to set up our night defensive perimeter (NDP). We quickly assumed our positions as

directed, placed our claymores, and prepared for darkness. Some gobbled cold c-rations, as warming them
would further compromise our position. One grunt whispered, "Gook." The whispering was passed on and we all
proned out. The gook had vanished with the knowledge
of our position. The night passed uneventfully. I felt
physically ill, but saddled up when ordered to do so. My
squad would not have point today. We would bring up
the rear.

* * *

Over my tour of duty, I would come to the personal conclusion that search-and-destroy missions, like the one I
had just experienced, was the sum total of the U.S.'s
strategy in Vietnam. Grunts would be inserted into the
jungle, and we would travel along until we found something, or something found us. We would then form a
skirmish line and move forward firing, letting the chips
fall where they may. Our search would be interrupted
periodically with the cumbersome tasks of calling in
firepower, getting resupplied, or taking on or removing
grunts for various reasons. Obviously, there was more to
it than this, but to grunts not privy to the "big picture,"
it felt like that's all we did.

Every new grunt went through a personal stumbling
phase. At this time, I was deeply involved in mine. I
pitied myself and knew I was the most miserable human

being alive on the planet. I could barely stand up, I couldn't eat c-rations, I couldn't shit, I couldn't communicate, sleep was difficult, and crying was out of the question. I found it impossible to function as a human being and knew I would soon cease to exist. There were just so many ways to get wasted that survival didn't seem possible. I would eventually adapt and become one with the jungle, but for now I was a liability, a real funny new guy. The experienced grunts would look at us and smile, probably recalling their own personal stumbling phases. Most would not give us a hard time, but would keep an eye on us, for their benefit.

I continued to absorb grunt language, including phrases like "It don't mean nothin'." This phrase could be applied to any situation, since nothin' meant nothin'. If a grunt found out he had to walk point that day, he could say "It don't mean nothin'." The same phrase could be used if a grunt received no mail when others did. Any time a grunt complained or made a comment to another grunt, the second grunt could answer with "There it is." "There it is" could mean thanks for stating the obvious or I understand you, my brother, and feel what you feel. A grunt had the right to call everybody else a "sorry ass mother fucker." Generally, though, this phrase was reserved for anybody higher up than the grunt saying it. Occasionally, it could be used on peers when they screwed up or, rarely, turned on one's self when it was obvious one had screwed up. And grunts never got angry, they'd get "a serious case of the ass."

That morning, Harry "Soup" Campbell learned he was going to be today's pointman:

Squad leader: "Soup, you got point today."

Soup: "Don't mean nothin'."

Squad leader: "There it is."

Soup to another grunt: "That sorry ass mother fucker has had a case of the ass for two weeks now."

Second grunt: "Don't mean nothin'. When I get wasted, bury me face down so the whole sorry ass world can kiss my ass, that sorry ass squad leader first."

The pointman was king for a day and was allowed an extra ration of a case of the ass. The point element generally consisted of the pointman himself, his slack-man, sometimes the squad leader, his RTO, a thump gunner (M-79), and a three-man machine-gun team. This order of march was constantly rearranged depending on terrain and enemy concentration. Generally the snake-like column was as effective as its point element. In ambush and booby trap situations, generally it was the point element that caught the shit and the rest of the column had no idea what was happening until it was over. In theory, you could have an entire battalion humping behind the point element with only the point element being effective. The costly strategy of getting on line and moving forward spewing tons of ammo could only be effective if the enemy held their position and let you shoot them. Quite often the enemy was satisfied with quickly destroying the point element and fleeing to avoid the on-line assault. If the Americans had other units set up in ambush mode, sometimes the fleeing enemy would be ambushed themselves. Occasionally, the enemy would hold their ground and fight for whatever reason. Perhaps they had a prized basecamp or weapon cache to defend or were ordered from higher ups to stand that day. The pointman was often involved in attempts to recover our killed-in-action. The U.S. had a policy of always trying to recover the bodies for family burial back in the world. Though well-intentioned, this policy was dangerous and cost many additional lives. For all these reasons the pointman job was less than a desirable one. There were other jobs you could take to avoid walking point. A grunt could carry the heavy PRC-25 radio or the heavy M-60 machine gun or be a thump-gunner. Usually the pointman was a rifleman and carried an M-16. Occasionally a thump-gunner or a machine gunner walked point, but that was rare. Some guys liked walking point for reasons all their own. Others were content to let them.

I had not arranged my fighting gear well and soon discovered an irritation on my right hip caused by my canteen rubbing against it. The irritation quickly grew into a huge, oozing, nasty-looking infection. I showed it to Frenchy who said, "Move that canteen, man, and get your shit together." Frenchy summoned the platoon medic, who was a black soldier from Louisiana. Naturally we all called him Doc. Doc went to work disinfecting and dressing the ugly mess. Each morning and evening, Doc would clean and re-dress the spot, and after about a week, it started to feel better. I still have a lemon-sized scar on my hip from the ordeal. Nobody wore underwear, as the rubbing fabric would cause irritation and infections.

It is impossible to convey in words the misery that mosquitoes, leeches, ticks, and other insects caused. We literally bathed in bug juice to protect ourselves, and to this day I hate the stuff. Ticks tended to find moist hairy spots to invade our blood streams. A direct hit of bug juice caused them to withdraw, and undoubtedly allowed bug juice access to our blood vessels. The ticks would be so pumped full of our blood, that their numerous legs were unable to connect with the ground. They had no chance of escape before we stomped them. They would explode, leaving a splatter of our own blood.

Doc was conscientious about caring for his grunts and dutifully passed out malaria pills each day. On Mondays, he passed out the huge Monday-Monday tablet, also for malaria, and watched each of us swallow it. These Monday-Mondays caused all kinds of weird action in our stomachs. A lot of guys claimed the pills kept them regular, but I think it was the c-rations we ate. Guys still caught malaria though. We lost more guys to malaria than in combat. Doc also passed out salt tablets to prevent dehydration. Initially, I took lots of salt tablets, but as my body acclimated to the jungle heat, I needed fewer and eventually stopped using them altogether.

I was still not feeling well and could barely keep up as the platoon moved on. A few days into the operation, around noon, the lieutenant called a chow break. The platoon just plunked down in place and the platoon sergeant sent out two, two-man listening posts, one to each flank of the column. I was placed with Frenchy on one flank approximately twenty metres from the column when I felt an urge I'd been waiting for. Nobody ever told me that grunts dug cat holes, took care of business, then covered it up to cut down on undesirable odours. I must have been foul due to my condition because guys back in the column became aware of the odour. Frenchy whispered, "Brown, cover it up, man, you are one foul dude." I was amazed at how light my step was now.

We humped till I thought I could hump no more, then we humped some more, and I knew I was one sorry ass mother fucker. We found an enemy trail and the lieutenant wanted to set up in ambush to try to get some. The trail was not fresh but it was the only one we had. We set up just adjacent to the trail in a five-position set. Three positions faced the trail, with a machine gun position at each end and one rifle position in the middle. The other two positions were rear security to cover our backside, where, of course, the lieutenant had his command position. In peacetime a platoon consisted of forty-four grunts; in Vietnam, I never saw a full platoon. We were operating with twenty-five guys at this time.

Our ambush site was on a little bank that was one metre higher than the trail. Frenchy set up his claymore in the middle of the bank and horizontal to the trail and told me to do the same. He had showed me how to reverse the wire on my claymore spool so I wouldn't have to unroll the whole spool to set it up each night. We screwed in the blasting caps and walked our wires back to the ambush position and hooked up our clackers (small electric generating devices).

"Frenchy dude, the back blast from our claymores will blow us all up," I said.

"Forget all that training shit," Frenchy said. "If we get gooks in the kill zone, the last thing to worry about is the back blast." In training, we had been taught to unroll the entire 100 metres of wire to be safe from the back blast. The claymores we had just set up were four metres from our position. Frenchy figured the bank would absorb the back blast.

With five guys in our position, some would pull guard twice and others would pull three one-hour guard shifts. Naturally, being an FNG, I got the three-shift deal. That night something happened to me that I am still ashamed of to this day. I broke grunt rule numero uno and a few minutes before guard change at 0300 hours, I fell asleep. The lieutenant was on guard in his rear position at the same hour, and there was no response from me on the radio to his call for our sit-rep (situation report). He threw rocks at me till I woke up. The next morning, I got blasted mercilessly.

"You little college fuckers are all the same," he said, with contempt. "Next time, I'll shoot you myself."

He was absolutely right, falling asleep on guard was unacceptable and there wasn't any excuse. I was guilty as heck and all I could say was, "It'll never happen again, sir." As punishment, I was banished to the rear of the platoon to hump just in front of Sergeant Hanes, who humped last and guarded our rear. Hanes was an E-6 shake 'n' bake type and a real nice guy. He kept pace, which meant he counted his steps and kept track of how many klicks we humped. Another aspect of my punishment was that, I too, had to count my steps. The lieutenant would check with Hanes to see if I could at least hump and count steps at the same time.

Hanes had recently returned from in-country training, where he had learned a new way of killing gooks. The Army taught Hanes, and then Hanes taught us, how to set up booby traps. The Army called them mechanical ambushes, and they were very effective. Basically, the idea was to set up claymores on a trail or expected avenue of enemy approach. Claymores were detonated with an electrical blasting cap and normally blown with the clacker, which had a charging handle on it. The charging handle, when depressed, generated about three volts of electricity, just enough to set off the electrical blasting cap, and therefore the claymore mine itself. In the mechanical ambush, a dry cell battery took the place of the clacker, supplying the voltage needed to detonate the claymore. A clothespin with metal conductors on each leg was wired to the battery and to the claymore itself. A piece of wood or plastic was then inserted between the two conductors on the clothespin, thereby breaking the circuit. A trip wire was then connected to the wood or plastic, and stretched across the trail at mid lower leg level. Everything would be set up prior to actually connecting the wire circuit to the battery, because when connected, the whole system was armed. The battery would then be hidden a safe distance from the kill zone. In two weeks' time, I would see the mechanical ambush used with alarming results.

Frenchy had recently told me the story of an eager platoon sergeant who thought he had the answer to the quick deployment of claymore mines. He had all the grunts connect up their claymores and carry them in their rucksacks, armed and ready to go. The idea was that when the claymore was needed it could be quickly placed on the ground. The grunts would then fall back, unravelling the wire as they went. His plan was soon abandoned when one grunt leaned back on his ruck on the jungle floor hard enough to depress his clacker. The explosion blew away that grunt, and two nearby grunts as well.

Our search for the elusive enemy continued and long daily humps led to more long daily humps. In peacetime a Ranger Battalion would have been manned by real Rangers, who would have all graduated from the Ranger School at Fort Benning, Georgia. This was Vietnam in late 1969; real Rangers in the battalion were rare, though there were still some. Several of the officers and shake 'n' bake NCOs were Ranger-qualified and they encouraged us to act like Rangers. Noise and light discipline procedures, for example, were strictly adhered to. Some of the Rangers, and some of the junior Rangers, wore the tiger-stripe fatigues by which the Rangers were known.

The battalion had a good reputation and lots of experienced people. Quite often, we operated in what were called re-enforced squads, a twelve-man team sent out on long-range patrols. Long-range patrols were usually seven- to ten-day-long operations. We humped heavy so we would not have to be resupplied. Getting resupplied meant a noisy rendezvous with a helicopter, which would then compromise our position. On these operations, we would carry half c-rations and half lurp rations, which are dehydrated rations that are light in weight. We would also carry eight to ten quarts of water, which was never enough for the entire operation. We would refill our canteens at stream crossings whenever possible. Sometimes the mission was to get to a blueline, a stream, just to get water so we wouldn't need to be resupplied.

On the long-range missions, we covered incredible distances. Daily humps of ten or twelve klicks were normal.

Occasionally, all teams of Bravo would link up at a common LZ to get resupplied. Any time that units linked up in the field, there was a real danger of mistaking each other for the enemy, and firefights between friendlies did occur. That's how Ordonez got a nasty scar on his left shoulder. Ordonez, a Puerto Rican from New York, was known as the best pointman in the platoon. He was walking point the day of a link-up. Then, the Rangers wore boonie hats, which resembled those of the enemy, instead of the distinctive steelpot helmets we wore now. As Ordonez approached for link-up, a fellow grunt at the LZ mistook him for a gook and fired him up. Luckily Ordonez only took one M-16 round to the fleshy tissue between his neck and upper shoulder. After that incident, the captain made everybody wear steelpots as headgear. We all hated wearing the heavy helmets, which couldn't stop a round from penetrating your skull anyway.

A grunt's existence in Vietnam has been described as long periods of boredom punctuated by moments of sheer terror. Though major battles had been fought in our AO with large-scale NVA units, we were not encountering the enemy in great numbers at this time. He was still out there, though, as we often heard firefights in the distance. Later, we would hear about the contact, and about how many Americans had been wasted. We all knew the distinctive sound of the AK-47 as it *clack, clack, clack*ed away. We all knew how the communist shoulder-fired rocket propelled grenade boomed when it was fired, and boomed again when it exploded. We had all seen booby traps, both large and small, and punji-stick pits the enemy dug around some of our most used LZs. Most of us were not looking for a fight, though, and would really have rather been home mowing the lawn.

I never heard one single grunt say, "I want to kick some commie ass, save the people of South Vietnam and end this war." Instead, grunts spoke of how many days they had left in their tours, and how they could hardly wait to get out of this mother fuckin' land. In order to fight effectively, soldiers need to believe in their mission and that victory is possible. None of the grunts I knew believed that. On long humps, my mind would wander, my thoughts melding into a hopeless mixture of feelings. All the while, unknowingly, I was forgetting about my old world of bright colour and spiralling down into this new world of drab green.

* * *

After a resupply link-up in a region of our AO called the Deadman area, the company set up platoon-size ambushes on the numerous hot trails. The three platoons were set up as close as 200 metres from each other. Sergeant Hanes had placed his mechanical ambush on the high-speed enemy trail near which we waited in ambush. The trail was wide, hard packed, and well travelled. The area was home to the c-61 Vietcong Company, who maintained many basecamps in the region. Around 0200 hours, I was jolted from my sleep by the closest, loudest boom I had ever heard. The entire platoon was alerted, and we assumed fighting positions, claymore clackers at the ready. I was in a rear security position and faced away from the trail. With heightened senses, and zero noise, we strained for sounds. We detected no movement and the word was whispered around that the claymores, strung together with detonation cord, had been detonated. It was completely dark that night so no squads were sent out to see what we got. We would wait for the light of dawn. Nobody slept much more.

Dunne and I were occupying the same nighttime fighting position and we quietly discussed what had happened. We both had two weeks in the field and had yet to see the enemy. The company CO was set up with another platoon on another trail a few hundred metres away and was delighted when he heard our platoon had blown away two gooks. In the morning, the CO and his platoon linked up with us after a squad from our platoon had reconned the kill zone and trail. The CO had his platoon set up a defensive perimeter around the kill zone and was rotating grunts through it so we could all get a good look at the dead gooks. Another E-6 sergeant in our platoon approached Dunne and me and said, "You FNGs get over there and see how gooks are supposed to look." Dunne and I obeyed the order and, with a few other grunts, went to see the carnage.

The scene is forever etched in my memory. Both were young, very beautiful Vietnamese women, approximately eighteen years old. They were very dead. Their legs had been severed just below the knees by the claymores and were nowhere to be found. They lay next to each other, eyes open and clouded. Both wore black pyjamas, and neither one seemed to have a weapon or ruck. Some grunts had opened their pyjama tops to expose young small breasts and pulled down their bottoms to expose small patches of pubic hair. One grunt walked by and pinched a small dark nipple, another ripped off his First Infantry Division patch and inserted it in a vagina with his knife, another walked by and threw an ace of spades on an exposed chest. The CO stood over the two women smoking and joking with his RTOs. As for me, I took Instamatic photos of the scene, which were later stolen by an REMF. I'm now thankful they were, and that I no longer possess them.

Dunne and I returned to our positions, unable to speak. Eventually he looked at me and said, "That's sick." I did not reply, as I sensed what would happen next. The E-6 that had ordered us to go look at the dead women, heard Dunne and went psycho on him.

"That's the enemy, you stupid fucker," he screamed, forgetting his noise discipline. "Get used to it, you'd better kill them before they kill you." Dunne did not reply, which pissed off the E-6 even more. He pushed Dunne, knocking him to the ground, and shouted, "Learn now or learn later, it's up to you."

Some grunts speculated that the Vietnamese girls were walking point for a much larger group of Vietcong who were on the move. The fact that the dead carried nothing tended to back up that scenario. VC had probably policed up the weapons and rucks, and then found another high-speed trail to use. Others thought they were travelling boom-boom girls moving from enemy basecamp to enemy basecamp entertaining the troops. That was also possible, but most favoured the first scenario. We left the dead where they were, no doubt winning the hearts and minds of the VC who would surely come looking for their girls. As the company moved out, artillery rounds rained down all over that trail network, just in case the enemy was still there.

* * *

Every five days or so, we would go back to Lorraine to secure the perimeter. Going to a firebase was like going to Disneyland in our world. We could get a shower, clean fatigues, receive mail, and, of course, smoke dew. Pot usage was widespread, and quietly tolerated, at least in line companies. One time, on a hump back to Lorraine, the company linked up at a large stream. The CO thought he'd let the boys have a swim. With a defensive perimeter in place, squads took turns in the water. When it was our squad's turn, Ordonez jumped right in, fatigues and all, and didn't notice when his bag of dew floated out of his cargo pocket. The CO saw the pot and chewed Ordonez out, but did not bust him. Grunts were needed in the field, not in Long Binh Jail. We didn't smoke openly, but we didn't try to hide it too much either. Some grunts smoked in the field but, generally, I restricted the practice to firebases and rear areas.

The dew was brought out to us on Lorraine by our "Kit Carson" scout. Kit Carson scouts were enemy soldiers who had switched sides and now were fighting against their old comrades. Each platoon travelled with one and, naturally, many grunts did not trust them. They wouldn't pull guard duty on firebases, but would return to Lai Khe, or wherever they went, come back, and sell drugs to the grunts. Our scout was doing well financially as he had a new Honda motorcycle in the rear to cruise around on.

About five months after I left Vietnam, a firebase in the American Division called Mary Ann would be overrun by a company of enemy sappers. They would kill thirty-two U.S. soldiers and wound eighty-two others in one of the most humiliating defeats the U.S. would ever suffer in Vietnam. Even back then in 1969, I knew that

Firebase Lorraine could have suffered the same fate. The firebase was relatively small, and at any one time I would have estimated troop strength to be approximately 150 guys. A well-executed ground attack could have done us a damn-damn, just like it would at Firebase Mary Ann. On firebases, we tended to feel safety in numbers, and thus our guard would come down a little.

I was getting stronger and adjusting to the heat, but I still felt very wronged. There were always alternatives open to drafted grunts who desperately wanted to get out of the field. The Army, for instance, gave us the option of re-enlisting and changing our jobs at any time. The downside was that we would be committed to the Army for another three years, starting from the day of the re-enlistment. It was hardly enticing. Many did re-enlist after short periods in the bush but I rejected the option outright. Also, around this time, there was a shortage of door gunners. If we agreed to extend our tours by six months, the Army would make us instant door gunners. Six more months in combat was also unappealing to me, so I decided to keep rolling the dice, and hope for the best.

We were sent back to operate in the Deadman area and were finding beaucoup booby traps on the trail network. Some of them were made with mackerel fish cans filled with explosives and detonated with GI-type blasting caps. The red fish cans were usually easy to see and the point element would mark them with toilet paper so the rest of the platoon would not trip them. On one trail there were so many of them, we couldn't blow them all up with our explosives. We moved a few hundred metres away and called in artillery strikes to destroy them.

The three platoons were operating apart from each other, but close enough to rapidly come to each other's aid. We were chowing down around noon, when we heard an enormous explosion. The single explosion was odd in that we were unaware of any friendly rounds being directed into our vicinity. The radio message came in and word spread: the platoon operating 300 metres away had tripped a major booby trap. There was one casualty and three wounded. We all quickly packed our rucks, saddled up, and prepared to move out to help. Then another radio message from the CO came in. We were to stay in place for now, as the affected platoon could handle their own dustoffs, or air medical evacuations, and because the area was rife with booby traps. "No shit, Captain," I thought to myself. We'd been tiptoeing around for days, afraid to move, sit, sleep, or breathe for fear of blowing ourselves up. Some of us wondered why we were still in this area, knowing that it was full of booby traps, but most knew the reason. The higher ups inserted us there in the hope of making contact with the enemy teams that had rigged them. It didn't settle well with the grunts, though.

The grunt who was killed by the explosion turned out to be George, a guy I had met back on Lorraine one night during a dew session. He was a fun guy and a well-respected pointman. He was blown away without a mark; the concussion got him. The grunts who'd been on scene later told us how George had had a very startled expression on his face as he groaned out the last breath in his young life. The booby trap that had killed George had been made using a dud American round. From where we were, we could hear the dustoff ship come in for the three wounded grunts, and there was yet another huge blast. The rotor wash from the dustoff had tripped another booby trap. This time there were no injuries. As we moved out from the area, we again heard hundreds of high explosive artillery rounds detonate in the booby-trapped region. Some of them would be dud rounds, no doubt, and they, too, would be booby-trapped by the resourceful enemy, thereby continuing the cycle of killing American kids with American rounds.

A few days later, we were airlifted to Lorraine to take our turn securing the firebase perimeter. We were told that there would be a company memorial service for George the next day at 1300 hours, then another air assault later in the afternoon. Naturally, as soon as we dropped our rucks, the pipes came out and were passed around. There was mail, cold Cokes, and partying.

The next day at the ceremony, we formed up just outside the wire, facing George's sixteen, which, with bayonet fixed, had been inserted into the ground. A GI steelpot, complete with flower power camouflage cover and band, rested on the butt of his sixteen facing our way. A pair of highly polished jungle boots stood at attention at the base. The lifeless symbol of the fallen soldier was not George, but it's all we had. The real George was on his way home. I didn't cry, but I felt cold in the heat and I had a serious case of goosebumps. There was the standard gun salute, and then the ceremony was over. The next order was, "Fall out, saddle up, and move out to the pad."

By the time of George's memorial, something had already happened deep inside me. Up until recently, I had been frozen with fear and hadn't been able to function properly. I'd been fading fast. Then, suddenly, a revelation had come over me in a surge of warmth and compassion. I hadn't willed it, it had just come. I realized that I would die in Vietnam and join the others that had died before me. It was the thought of joining the others that gave me the most peaceful sensation I'd experienced in my twenty years of life. It was instant relief and my health improved immediately. I could sleep again, I could eat, poop, pee, chuck 'n' jive with the other grunts, and feel alive again. I knew what I had to do: relax when nothing was happening, the fear would return all by itself when required.

* * *

We assembled on the pad as ordered. The slicks arrived to lift us to a region of the AO our squad had not yet been in. We were again operating in the twelve-man re-enforced squad configuration. The operations were again longer, the seven- to ten-day deal. The Army had a new plan to kill gooks, called the "flip-flop operation." A twelve-man squad from Charlie Company had been operating in the area for about a week. Part of the plan was for that squad to be noisy and draw attention to themselves, which apparently they had done. The Charlie Squad was set up in the tree line adjacent to the LZ, as our squad was inserted on two slicks as close to the tree line as possible. As the slicks touched down, Charlie's team immediately moved out of the tree line toward the landing slicks and we moved quickly toward their old position. The teams crossed paths as they were extracted and we were inserted. The plan was to make the enemy believe the GIs operating there had been extracted. Our plan obviously required that our insertion be undetected. We were very silent and we immediately proned out in a tight circular perimeter. With rucksacks off, we waited silently to see what would develop.

I was the only one who saw them. I was proned out, facing away from the LZ. Everyone else must have been looking toward the LZ, expecting that's where the enemy would come from. I saw two scruffy-looking VC carrying weapons and rucksacks, walking away from our tight circle. How they had got there, without somebody seeing them, was beyond me, and how had they not seen us? I had to act quickly as they were moving away. I very quickly glanced at the grunts closest to me to try to get their attention, but I couldn't make eye contact. I had to do something. I flipped my selector to the semi-auto position, raised up on one knee, drew a bead on the VC on the left and started squeezing off rounds. One round, two rounds, and then *click*, as my sixteen double-fed and ceased to fire. I quickly pulled back the charging handle only to jam a third round into the first two. My sixteen was jammed big-time. The other grunts turned to see the gooks perform the quickest rucksack dismount exit stage straight-ahead manoeuvre ever done. The gooks must have practised that one. Everybody opened up, and I watched as the VC ran for their lives. Somebody shouted, "Cease fire," and grunts jumped up and ran after the fleeing gooks. One grunt threw me a 4-inch .38 calibre Smith & Wesson revolver saying, "Here, use this." I stayed right there. Chasing gooks down a trail didn't seem like a cool thing to do. The other grunts returned quickly, apparently realizing running down gook trails was not too tactical either. They scooped up the two rucks, returned to our circle, and radioed in what had happened.

The Battalion Commander, himself, heard the radio message and ordered us to hold our position. He wanted to come out to the LZ and get the rucksacks. We wanted to didi mau before those guys came back with a bigger and badder gang than ours. We maintained a tight, nervous circle and waited for the big grunt in the sky to arrive. While we waited, I tried to unjam my sixteen. The rounds were so stuck, I had to use pliers and pull with force to get it freed up. I never trusted an M-16 again. The commander must have been at the girlfriend's hootch in Lai Khe because it took him half an hour to get there. One grunt ran the rucks out to the landing helicopter, and the big guy was gone.

Orders came from higher up to recon the trail the gooks had run down. There were no officers on the team that day. The senior NCO, an E-5 shake 'n' bake, was getting short and did not like the idea of reconning the trail. We quickly saddled up and moved toward our right flank. Away from the trail and LZ, we were looking for a hole to hide in. About one klick later, we found the perfect place. The vegetation had thickened and we found a clump of thick bamboo surrounded by many other thick clumps of thick bamboo. We silently set up our perimeter, placing our claymores in real tight, and we laid up real quiet. We stayed put two nights and called in phoney reports about the recons that we were supposed to be running. It was never advisable to stay anywhere two nights, but we were well hidden and were happy to lay up. We knew, eventually, we'd be checking that trail, which we did after our self-given two-day in-country R&R.

We whispered back and forth, discussing the contents of the abandoned rucks, which we had examined before we handed them over. They had contained

GI c-rations, approximately fifty rounds of U.S.-made 7.62mm ammunition, numerous papers that we could not translate, and worn ratty personal photos of girl-friends and family members. The c-rations had all had a machete-size gash through them. The contents were rotten, and maggots crawled all over the cans and ruck-sacks. When we got resupplied in the field, the REMFs, quite often, would send too many cases of c-rations. Nobody wanted to hump the extra weight, so we'd punch a hole in each can so the contents would rot, thus depriving the enemy of a free lunch. Obviously, the two VC we had seen hadn't minded eating maggots with their beans and weenies.

We weren't sure how the VC had got the U.S. ammo, but we had some ideas. Each grunt humped 100 rounds of 7.62mm linked machine-gun ammo. Every night the linked ammo would be handed over to the machine gunners in case they needed it through the night. If not used, each grunt would reclaim his 100 rounds the next morning in preparation for the day's hump. With the daily passing back and forth of the ammo belts, 100 rounds could conceivably be left behind. (I didn't want to believe that a grunt would deliberately leave his 100 rounds behind to lighten his load.) The resourceful enemy soldiers could easily follow along behind a sloppy platoon and scoop up lost or forgotten ammo, grenades and claymores; feed themselves on the garbage; and pick up and use whatever else the GIs had left. Williams had told me to never leave behind an envelope with a read-able return address. The enemy had, in the past, written letters to loved ones using the left-behind address. The enemy would inform loved ones of the death or capture of the GI, causing extreme grief to the family.

It's very dangerous to call in false positions, but that second night in the bamboo clump, we did just that. The short E-5 didn't want to move yet, and none of the other grunts wanted to either. There was a lot of discussion about our not moving and its obvious dangers, but all agreed that it was better to stay put for now, and hope that our own artillery gunners didn't blow us away. Besides, we all figured, when mortar, rocket, or artillery rounds explode, the shrapnel goes up and out. It would take a direct hit for the concussion to blast us. We slept soundly, confident in our decision to hole up.

The next day, our vacation was over; we had to check out the trail the gooks had used for their hasty escape. We quietly disarmed our claymores, packed up our rucks, saddled up and moved out. The team, well spread out, slowly headed for the LZ using a different route than the one we had used two days before; we were all definitely keeping in mind the strong possibility of an enemy ambush. We located the trail, but the point element, reluctant to invite ambush, paralleled where possible. At times, the vegetation was super thick, and we had to hump on the spooky trail itself. There were trails every-where – big ones, little ones, paralleling ones. Crossing at intersections was done as strategically as possible.

It took hours to hump one klick, which was about the point where Daly found his cool war trophies. Daly, a grunt from Illinois, was humping mid-team and had seen something that caught his eye. It was an old, rotten, hollowed-out tree trunk, approximately two feet in diameter. The vegetation in the hollow trunk looked out of place, as if it wasn't fresh, and it leaned against the trunk in an unnatural way. Daly whispered for us to halt, and, alone, approached the trunk. He cautiously lifted the unnatural vegetation and peered inside. It was a mini weapon cache containing one fully operational, well maintained, SKS rifle, a communist weapon that fired 7.62mm ammo, the same as the American M-14 or M-60 machine gun. There was also an NLF Vietcong flag in dandy shape. Naturally, we were all jealous of his find. He would take his trophies home.

We knew there was a basecamp in the area, but we were unable to find it. The Vietnamese had been fighting various imperialists for centuries and had learned how to hide basecamps very well. One common thread, however, was that even the Vietnamese needed water and many basecamps were located close to streams. Some older, established ones had dug out shallow wells away from streams.

On one platoon-size operation, while walking point, I stumbled into an unoccupied bunker complex. I was just about on top of the first bunker before I realized it.

Neither the complex nor the trail, which I thought was an animal path, were fresh. When I realized what I had stumbled upon, I immediately assumed the facedown grunt position. When the pointman drops, everybody drops, so the entire platoon proned out. Williams was walking slack for me and he said, "Brown, get up. There hasn't been a dink around here for months." I was slightly embarrassed and received a lot of chiding from the other grunts who were as relieved as I was. We quickly destroyed the bunkers by hand. We didn't want to use C-4 explosive, which would have drawn attention to ourselves. The bunkers were simple – they were holes that had been dug out, roofed over with six- to ten-foot-long trees that had been cut by hand and then covered with dirt from the hole. There were no firing ports; it was a place to ride out American firepower. If anything dropped from the sky, the enemy could hop in and wait for the firestorm to pass.

Around this time, we received some FNGs even newer than Dunne and I. They were deeply involved in their personal stumbling phases, while Dunne and I were somewhat acclimatized. Sergeant Hanes, as was his habit, was deploying nightly mechanical ambushes. He used new guys to pull security while he set up his booby traps. Dunne and I, being graduates of his jungle warfare schooling, helped lay out the wires, claymores, and trip wire and would camouflage the components. Hanes would make sure everyone knew exactly where the trip wire was so no accidents would occur the next morning. As usual, we dropped back while Hanes hooked up the battery. The next morning, the team went out to disarm the system. Hanes had one of the FNGs walk point to the location and asked, "Are you sure you remember where the trip wire is?"

"Yeah, yeah, I'm not stupid," the FNG replied.

Hanes told me to walk slack and keep an eye on the FNG. I knew exactly where the trip wire was, as I always used a point of reference, such as a specific tree, rock, or bush. As we approached the bush I had used as a marker, my eyes focused on the barely visible wire. It was taut, and straight lines do not occur naturally in the jungle. The stupid FNG did not slow his pace. I yelled, "Freeze." He froze with his right lower leg just touching the wire. I assumed the prone position, and so did the other grunts. I told him to back up, which he did. Hanes disarmed the thing and we all kept an eye on that FNG from then on.

* * *

Christmas was approaching, and we all got invited to Lai Khe to see Bob Hope entertain the troops. Naturally, we would have to clear the "rocket belt" region of our area of operation first; it would be bad press if Bob Hope got wasted by a rocket delivered from our AO. Around mid-December, then, Alpha and Bravo Companies began operating platoons around the rocket belt region. We were airlifted to the region, which, as I recall, was double-canopy jungle. We humped for days and eventually found an unoccupied rocket-launching site. The bamboo tripods used for launching were still in place. There were empty crates and metal containers strewn about, but no rockets or enemy rocket teams were found. There was little doubt, however, a rocket with Bob Hope's name on it could have been launched from that site. A platoon from Alpha Company had much better results. The night before the show, they engaged eight enemy soldiers at an established launch site. Alpha Rangers killed two enemy soldiers and captured one. Three ready rockets aimed at Lai Khe were, no doubt, laid on for the Bob Hope Christmas show of 1969.

We were extracted 21 Dec 69 and flown back to Lorraine. We secured the perimeter that night, and departed the following morning by truck for Lai Khe. The mood was more than festive as we smoked and joked on the trucks. The boys were going to town, a rare treat for line company grunts. The show was in the afternoon, so we had a few hours to kill. We were ordered to leave all weapons under guard in an area laid out for the company. Williams, street- and bush-smart as he was, said, "Fuck that shit. We're grunts, put one frag in each cargo pocket." So I, along with some others, concealed fragmentation grenades and went to see what was up. Williams, Frenchy, and I went to the village located in the centre of the basecamp. The fenced-off ville was full of bars, shops, steam baths, and all the honky-tonk stuff set up to extract cash from GIs. We went into a bar that was overrun with boom-boom girls demanding that we buy them Saigon tea at exorbitant prices. The tea was non-alcoholic sugar water that GIs bought for the girls just to spend time with them. Actual boom-boom, of course, was available. I was not uninterested, just intimidated. Vietnamese girls could be attractive but they looked ridiculous wearing the culturally incorrect dress and makeup of Western hookers. I passed on the boom-boom and browsed around the numerous trinket shops instead.

Eventually, we drifted over toward the area set up for the show, still armed with concealed grenades. There were 15,000 guys grouped tightly together to see Bob Hope. From where we stood, we could barely see the stage, let alone the show. We all joked about the substantial REMF representation and how one rocket would make the war real for them. We smoked dew and were happy not to be humping the boonies. Bob opened with prepared jokes: "So, this is Lai Khe – well, I just got here and me no likee." He went on, "We're so close to the fighting, we had to give the Vietcong half the tickets." The guests were Neil Armstrong, Connie Stevens, Suzanne Charney, *Laugh-In*'s Teresa Graves, the Gold Diggers, Miss World 1969, and of course, Les Brown and his band of renown. The show was filmed and aired back in the world. Nancy later wrote to me, after seeing the show on television with her family, about how her little brother, Ritchie, had screamed in delight, "I knew it, I knew it, I knew we'd see Les Brown." He was referring to the grunt Les Brown, and not the band leader.

The GIs rotating into the war system brought with them the most current cultural characteristics of society back home. At this point in the war, drafted grunts brought anarchy, dissent, drug usage, rebellion, and disgust for a war that had dragged on much too long without hope of moving forward. To say the U.S. Army had a discipline problem would be the understatement of the century. Individuals and even whole companies were refusing battle orders blatantly. The fragging of officers who were viewed by grunts to be dangerous to grunts' safety was happening all over the war zones. "Fuck the Army," abbreviated to FTA, was highly visible everywhere in graffiti displayed on helmet art, trucks, signs, buildings, and anywhere else possible. Troops consumed alcohol, drugs, both soft and hard, and grew their hair as long as they could get away with. Uprisings in rear areas reflected uprisings back in the world.

GIs of all races were brothers in the bush, but in rear areas, racial groups tended to keep to themselves, just like they did back home. I was hangin' with Williams and Frenchy, who were both black. Black and white REMFs would stare in disgust wondering, "What's wrong with those guys."

That night after the show, we slept on the ground in tents erected for our one-night stay in civilization. Most of us couldn't sleep on cots or bunks anyway; we were out of the habit. That night, a rumour spread quickly that one boom-boom girl had escaped through the village's wire and was taking on Bravo Rangers, one at a time, for five bucks. Some estimates were as high as fifty guys dipping their wicks. I did not participate. The thought of standing in line with my pants down and five dollars military payment currency at the ready was more than unappealing. At the end of the line, apparently, a grunt had dipped his wick, retrieved his five bucks, and everybody else's five bucks, then had beat the shit out of the boom-boom girl. More hearts and minds were won that night for sure.

The following morning, we were trucked back to Lorraine, and the next day, we airlifted back to the Deadman region in a company-sized assault. Our platoon went in first, secured the LZ, and the slicks made two more sorties bringing in the rest of the company. The platoons moved out in different directions searching for the elusive enemy. They were laying low, perhaps waiting for Vietnamization to occur, at which time they would then again dominate the area.

Vietnamization was Nixon's plan to have us equip and train the ARVNs, in preparation for our eventual withdrawal, while at the same time bombing the shit out of North Vietnam. Rumours about the withdrawal of the entire First Infantry Division were rampant. No doubt, the enemy knew more about the withdrawal than those of us actually in the First Infantry Division. The rumours added to our reluctance to make contact. The enemy must have been thinking the same thing: "Why take on the Americans now? They're leaving, we'll wait and kick ass on the wimpy ARVNs." Guys were giggling like schoolgirls at the thought of going home early, and as victors to boot.

We were in the Deadman region, but not the highly booby-trapped area of before. This area had natural clearings large enough to airlift battalions in and out. We were linked up to company size for a Christmas turkey dinner. Cooks from Lorraine had accompanied the field chow containers, and had set up a buffet line. I didn't trust jungle-cooked turkey and had by this time grown accustomed to eating c-rations and lurp rations. That's the trouble with those Army rations – at first you can't eat them and then after a while, you can't eat anything else. I had my personal favourites and would trade with other grunts to obtain them. The Army had what they called heat tabs, which we were supposed to use to warm up our meals. The damn things emitted such noxious fumes that grunts refused to use them. Frenchy showed me how to take a small chunk of c-4 explosive, shape it into a cone, and voilà, instant gas range for barbecuing c-ration pork slices or making hot chocolate from the powder they gave us. Frenchy's warning was stern. "Once the C-4 is burning, never ever stomp on it to put it out. We had a grunt blowed half his foot off that way." My all-time favourite grunt meal was the dehydrated lurp ration chicken and rice. If prepared properly with just a dash of Worcestershire sauce and Tabasco, it was to die for. Of course, weenies and beans with a B-2 unit of cheddar cheese melted into the can was hardly a beggar's banquet. Food was a personal issue. Grunts carried as much or as little as they desired.

Any time an operation was extended by the higher ups, we called it a "rat fuck." An operation could be five days at the beginning, get rat-fucked twice, and end up being a fifteen-day operation. On one rat-fucked operation, I had humped just enough food for five days. A resupply was scheduled for the sixth day. The resupply got rat-fucked because the slicks were busy on some other, more important operation. My shit was weak because I was out of rations and water on the fifth day. Guys were pissin' and moanin' about being hungry and thirsty. We were miserable, though not starving to death. Williams flipped me half a quart of water and a can of spaghetti and said, "Here, always keep some extra shit on hand for the rat fucks."

The Christmas dinner slicks had brought us not only the turkey special, but some replacements as well. We got a brand-new butter-bar second lieutenant to be our new platoon leader. This was my third lieutenant in as many months. The lieutenant that had deservedly chewed my ass out for falling asleep on guard duty was, shortly after that, replaced by another lieutenant, who was now being replaced by this lieutenant. Officers were supposed to serve six months in the field while we enlisted trash served twelve months. I guess the higher ups kept them rotating out to make sure they didn't learn anything, or that the enlisted trash didn't frag 'em. To be fair, I did serve under some competent, as well as incompetent, leaders. Our new lieutenant was a nice guy, drafted like me, and trying to make the best of a shitty set of circumstances. I got to know him because I was the platoon radio telephone operator at this time. I had been walking point for democracy when "Frog," the regular RTO, went on R&R. After two and a half months of walking point, I figured I needed a less spooky job and volunteered to hump Frog's radio. Frog was a big strong white grunt from Louisiana, so naturally we treated his radio as if it was his very own. He gave me a twenty-minute crash course on it and said, "I expect to find this radio in the same shape it's in now when I get back." He taught me radio procedures, battery replacement, how to clean the handset connections, and how to protect the handset from the unbelievable monsoon rains. It weighed over twenty pounds, and I also had to hump two heavy spare batteries.

As platoon RTO, I was now a member of the command position (CP), which consisted of the lieutenant, his RTO, the medic, and platoon sergeant. The neat thing about humping the radio is you know what the heck is going on; the bad points are the burdensome weight of the radio and the fact that you're a walking target for enemy snipers. As platoon RTO, I started to learn more about things like calling in and directing artillery and air strikes, and about our missions and where we were. Up to this point, I hadn't ever looked at a map of where we were operating. Generally, the maps were accurate and gave high-quality information about possible landing zones, bluelines, and so on.

On a twelve-grunt mission during that operation, we found a really good hiding place to set up for the night. We felt secure, as we had not seen the enemy for weeks. After setting up our perimeter, Williams motioned for me to come over to his position. I had Doc monitor the radio for me and went to see what was up. Williams smiled, broke out his bowl and dew, and fired it up. I guess the lieutenant smelled the odour of burning pot and liked it cause he came right on over and passed the bowl with us. We all giggled with our eyes, so as not to make any noise. That was the first and last time I ever got high with an officer.

Doc had also gone on R&R, so they had given us a replacement. The new Doc was a conscientious objector and carried no weapon. It was odd to see a GI humping the boonies unarmed and I asked Doc what was up with that. He told me that he had been drafted and that he had told the Army he was non-violent and would not kill. The Army told him they had the perfect job slot for him, and that's how he became a medic. Doc said, "When the shit hits the fan, an M-16 just gets in the way of my work anyway." I and others truly respected the dude. He was honouring his military obligations on his own terms. One night, the new Doc started dippin' into the medicine chest, and got a serious case of the loud giggles. I had to get him to hush up but the more I tried, the more he giggled. He was bustin' his guts with laughter, and it was contagious, cause I, too, started to giggle. Soon, there was a clusterfuck of giggling grunts. Eventually, we stopped giggling and things got more tactical. All through the night, Doc would intermittently resume his giggling. Maybe Doc had it all figured out, and the joke was on us.

We had a Hispanic grunt from Texas in the platoon, who was anxious to zap some gooks. At night, sometimes he would have serious nightmares that resulted in screaming and throwing his body to and fro. The nearest grunt would have to wake him up to get him to chill out. One day, the Texan, who carried an M-79 grenade launcher, was humping behind me when he had an accidental discharge. Luckily, the thump gun was pointed straight up when he fired the high-explosive round. I passed the word up and down the column to "Hold up" while we waited for the round to come back down. No one was hurt, but it was an awful feeling not knowing whether to shit or go blind. Eventually, Frog and our regular Doc returned from R&R, so I was off the radio.

It was now my turn to hump ammo for one of the two machine-gun teams in the platoon. The machine-gun team consisted of three grunts: the gunner, the assistant gunner, and the ammo bearer. The gunner, obviously, actually fired the M-60 machine gun, the assistant gunner guided and fed the belted ammo into the firing weapon, and the ammo bearer carried the one thousand rounds of belted ammo in two steel ammo boxes. The lowest job for a grunt in Vietnam was being an ammo bearer. The weight of the ammo was outrageous. When freshly resupplied, many ammo bearers were unable to stand without assistance. The task was so arduous, that grunts were sentenced to only sixty days, because that's all a human body could handle. An ammo bearer is afforded an extra ration of "a case of the ass" because his complaints are justified.

I was humpin' ammo, up front with Daly's machine gun, when I heard Williams, the pointman, fire his sixteen. I immediately assumed the facedown grunt position, as did the other grunts, except Daly, my gunner. He was gung-ho, so rather than proning out, he immediately ran forward past Williams and crouched down behind a bush. He turned and hollered, "Brown, get up here with the ammo." I slipped out of my ruck and dutifully ran up with knees bent and body hunched over as much as possible. I stopped next to Williams, who looked like he was high. "I got the mother fucker," he mumbled to me.

I ran up to Daly's position and quickly hooked up to his gun. From there, I could see a small clearing in the jungle. It was not a natural clearing; it was obvious the trees had been chopped down. From where I was, I couldn't see any bunkers, and we were not taking fire. A few more grunts moved up to the gun position. We got on line and moved forward.

I could now see who Williams had hit. He was down, looking our way, with an arm raised and an open hand, in the form of the universal "I'm hurt, I surrender" position. As we approached the wounded gook, the Texan broke ranks and ran up to fire two rounds from his .45 calibre handgun into the gook's head.

The rest of the team arrived and we found one newly constructed bunker. It was a basecamp under construction, as we could see other bunkers that were partially completed. We didn't see other enemy soldiers. Ordonez threw a frag in the bunker. Then, he stripped off all his gear, including his fatigue shirt, and had somebody tie a rope to his waist. Armed with a flashlight and a .45 calibre handgun, he crawled in through the small entrance. He came out quickly and told us, "It's clear." Ordonez had found numerous documents and the big daddy of souvenirs, a Chicom 9mm handgun. It was black, and had twin red stars on the pistol grips. Since Ordonez had searched the bunker, he got to keep his trophy.

The dead gook seemed totally out of place. He wore a freshly laundered light blue dress shirt, neatly pressed tan trousers, and clean polished street shoes. As was almost always the case, we were in a free fire zone, so he had to be the enemy in some capacity or other.

We were operating in the twelve-man grunt config-uration so we were anxious to didi mau before the dead gook's buddies came back. We saddled up and moved off in a direction dictated to us by the higher ups. We trav-elled quickly, but cautiously, to put some distance between us and the basecamp. We found a good hiding place but this time humped past it for a couple hundred metres in order to create a trail. We then moved back on our own trail and entered the thick clump of vege-tation. Daly's machine gun was placed facing our freshly made trail. The grunts each handed over their 100 rounds of linked ammo and I organized it all for quick feed. Some grunts went back out on our trail and set up mechanical ambushes at both ends of the kill zone; clay-mores around the perimeter were placed in tight. We didn't smoke any dew that night, as we settled in to see what would develop. Just before dawn, the mechanical ambush at the end of the kill zone, towards the base-camp, detonated. We were all alerted to the explosion. We heard no other sounds. After the sun had been up for an hour, five riflemen went to check our trail. I stayed in place with Daly's gun.

The squad returned with news of another dead gook. They didn't find any weapons or personal effects. We saddled up and cautiously moved out in the direction of an LZ where we were to be extracted. We found the natural clearing, which was large enough for one slick to land, right where it was supposed to be. The pilot of the lead slick radioed for us to pop smoke, which we proceeded to do. The purple smoke rose through the air, and the pilot expertly guided his craft and touched down. Six grunts ran from the tree line, boarded the slick, and skyed up. I was going on the next lift, as it was always advisable to extract the machine-gun team last. As the second slick approached, I could see two Cobra gunships stalking about with their painted-on sharks' teeth clearly visible. Safely extracted, we were on our way to our new firebase, known as "Dominate."

At the firebase, the bowls came out quicker than usual, as we mellowed out and discussed the operation. Naturally, the documents we had found were handed over to the higher ups and, of course, information did not come back down to us. So we made up our own scenarios, and came to our own conclusions. We all thought that the first dead VC was high-ranking. His 9mm Chinese communist handgun drew us to that conclusion. We could not come up with a reason for him being there, dressed as he was. Some thought he was a honcho adviser to the local VC clan; others thought he might be some kind of spook playing both sides of the game. The second VC, we thought, was probably the pointman for a group stalking our squad. Perhaps he had seen our trail in the distance, unaware that we were lying in ambush.

The fact that we found no weapon or personal effects led us to believe other VC had policed up the stuff and split.

Some of the grunts were pissed off about the Texan finishing off the honcho VC, execution style. Many felt we should have patched him up and taken him prisoner to find out what he was up to. Nobody said anything to the Texan though. To do so would have been contrary to the unwritten grunt rules. Nobody said anything to the higher ups, either; that was never even a consideration. The Texan's nightmares were severe enough to have gotten him out, but he wanted to stay and kill gooks. I guess every platoon needed a few guys like that around.

I was shocked when Daly approached me and told me, "I expect you to stay with my gun. When I move, you move."

"Man," I replied, "when I hear rounds being capped off, I drop till I know what's goin' on. I'll move then; I suggest you do the same."

We heard later that Charlie Company Rangers were inserted, company size, in the area, but no contact was made. The enemy was apparently just as reluctant to fight as we were, for the withdrawal rumours were more rampant than ever.

Dominate was still under construction but the guns were in place. Some bunkers and fighting positions were completed, but the spooky aspect of the place was the surrounding tree line, which was thick double-canopy jungle. The distance from the perimeter to the tree line was only about 300 metres. Lorraine had been located in an area that had been cleared of trees for kilometres in all directions.

The U.S. Army was not known for its tree-hugging characteristics, as huge areas of forest and jungle were defoliated to deprive the enemy of hiding spots. The Army used "roam plows" to clear sections in well-defined grid patterns. The roam plows were the biggest, meanest bulldozer-like machines known to mankind. A bunch of roam plows would get on line moving forward together, knocking down every living thing in their path. Chemical defoliants (some of which were supplied by Canadian chemical companies) were also used in liberal doses. Our area of operation had been devastated by years of exploding ordnance delivered by land guns, Navy sea guns, and bombs dropped from the air. Everywhere we humped, we would see huge trees down and splintered from exploding steel.

* * *

Our operations out of "Dominate" were mostly unproductive. There were certainly signs of recent enemy activity, but the enemy chose not to make contact. Around this time, rumour had it that the entire First Infantry Division was going to be withdrawn from Vietnam mid-April 1970, to be replaced by the Fifth ARVN Division. On one operation, the Army assigned an entire company of ARVN soldiers to our platoon. Apparently, they were to learn from us, but all we wanted to do was get away from them. The ARVN company was fat as we counted over one hundred soldiers. At night, they would set up in a company clusterfuck with no semblance of order or security. In the middle of the clusterfuck would be a huge cooking fire complete with a large black pot for rice. They laughed loudly, joked, cooked, and sang songs. It looked to us like they were on some sort of group picnic. We all thought these sorry ass dudes were gonna soon get their asses kicked, so they might as well party now. More likely, the ARVNs knew what was going on with the lack of contact and felt safe for the moment. Besides, the Americans were still around to rescue them if need be, so no worries for now. Eventually, the higher ups bent to our wishes and we parted ways with the ARVNs.

The higher ups did not take any pressure off us, as rat fucks were the norm and operations sometimes lasted up to twelve or fifteen days. Being unclean, for that length of time in those conditions, led to all kinds of nasty jungle-rot skin problems. Guys had sores that oozed pus, mostly on the arms. Doc would treat us as best he could. Some guys would be infected all over and would have to be sent to Lai Khe for drug treatments and scrubbings to clear up the mess. Sometimes, a grunt would develop a super high fever, and Doc would send him in. It always turned out to be the same thing: malaria. He'd be gone for a few weeks then reappear on a resupply helicopter.

I honestly believed I was going home, and was temporarily happy. Rumours started coming down that guys with less than six months' in-country would be reassigned to other divisions. My calculations put me at about six and a half months in-country at the time of withdrawal, so I thought I was safe. New rumours followed and the time-in-country factor kept changing, so after a while, I didn't know what to expect. I should have been more suspicious. I was in the U.S. Army, after all.

Around February 1970, the Bravo Rangers received a three-day stand-down in the rear. I forget how we got there, but we ended up at the in-country stand-down centre back at Di An. There were dreaded haircuts and shot-record updates as well as partying. The centre even had a miniature golf course set up for the kids to play on. I thought to myself, "Jesus H. Christ, I am not the least bit interested in playing anything, let alone mini-putt." I was an eighty-year-old man in a twenty-one-year-old body. I never saw one grunt playing miniature golf. I did, however, see beaucoup bored REMFs joking and playing on the course set up for grunts. Grunts were mostly drunk and high and worried about where they'd send us next. We were trained, nomadic warriors. We were so mobile that in a matter of minutes after receiving a saddle-up command, we'd be on our feet, with all our possessions on our backs, ready to board trucks, airplanes, boats, or helicopters. We seldom slept in the same place two nights. I was tired of continuously being on the move and wanted to settle down and make a stand. I thought, "Give me a bunker to call home, and I will defend it with my life, but let me stay in one place for a while."

Frenchy, Williams, and I were shootin' the bull one day when the topic of drafted or enlisted came up. I was surprised to learn that both of them had enlisted but I didn't ask them why. When I told them I was a Canadian draftee, they were shocked and couldn't believe it. "You're shittin' me, man, that's gotta be fuckin' illegal," Williams said. I explained to them the draft rules for legal alien permanent residents, but they never did believe me. Sometimes, when it was time to move out, they'd say, "Okay now, saddle up, Canuck."

After the three days of debauchery, we were immediately sent back to the bush lest we get used to being REMFs. Again, we operated out of Dominate, making no contact with the VC. The Army even sent us a dog tracking team to sniff out the enemy. The dog, a German Shepherd, was well disciplined and never made a sound. He wore a concerned expression on his face, just like the rest of the grunts. The dog handler carried rations and water for his dog and showered him with affection. I envied their relationship. That dog could walk through dried jungle vegetation without making a sound. He was a professional. He did not, however, find any gooks. Maybe he had heard the rumours and wanted to go home as well.

* * *

Near the end of February the Battalion was again on the move. We were airlifted to Lai Khe, then boarded c-130 fixed-wing aircraft bound for, I think, Bien Hoa. It was a huge operation. Battalions were on the move in a last effort to clear out the last of the Vietcong before Vietnamization. We were assembled on a huge airstrip with thousands of troops. The Air Force crews were obviously nervous with all us ammo-heavy grunts boarding their airplanes. The Air Force guys didn't want any accidental discharges, so they checked each weapon to ensure it was cleared. We all laughed as we boarded with frags, LAWs, handguns, claymores, c-4, white phosphorus grenades, and various weapons of mass destruction.

Word of Ordonez's souvenir Chicom 9mm handgun spread quickly to the assembled aircrews. They approached our platoon area in small groups and tried to buy or trade for it. Ordonez sent them all packing.

"Volunteer to be a grunt and get your own," he told them all.

One Cobra gunship pilot thought he had what Ordonez wanted.

"I'll take you for a ride in my Cobra and let you fire the mini guns," he offered.

"Get the fuck outta here, fly boy," Ordonez replied. "Your aftershave is lingering and the gooks will know where I am."

Bravo Rangers would be operating company-size, as rumour had it we were to assault a known enemy base-camp. Our platoon went in first. We secured the LZ and the other two platoons came in. The LZ was cold, but gunships orbited all around anyway, poised to strike. It was late afternoon. We left the LZ single file, about sixty-five grunts in a snake column. Our platoon brought up the rear. We moved only a few hundred metres from the LZ, crossed a blueline, and set up a defensive circular perimeter. I was assistant gunner to Frenchy, who had recently taken over Daly's gun, and Dunne was our ammo bearer. While we organized our position, I noticed that Dunne was lethargic and didn't look so good. He said, "I feel like dog shit, man. I don't know what's wrong with me."

As I looked up, I saw a grunt was pointing across the stream. He whispered, "Gook." I observed one VC dressed in dark clothing and a boonie hat, carrying the distinctive AK-47 with a banana magazine. When the VC saw that he'd encountered an entire infantry company, he turned and ran. The vegetation was somewhat open, we were not hidden at all. Grunts chased across the stream, and I followed. The gook was long gone. We found a well-worn trail, but reluctant to invite ambush, we did not move forward on it. The trail started just across the stream from our position. We would later figure out that it was the footpath used by the enemy to get water to supply the basecamp. The enemy now knew our exact numbers and location, but we did not know his. The CO ordered up a 50 per cent guard. I figure he got almost 100 per cent that night. The night passed uneventfully, and the next day our platoon was selected to follow the trail. Another platoon moved up the stream to cross. The third platoon, and the CO, would stay in place as a reaction force. The CO sent his artillery lieutenant forward observer, the FO, with us.

Our platoon's point element crossed the stream and slowly moved on the trail. The forward movement was so slow, that it seemed we stood still more than we moved forward. The hours passed, and we had only moved approximately 400 metres. From our position in the column, we could never see the point. The trail itself was very well used, and long-time traffic and erosion had made it lower than ground level. The trail abruptly veered right and we now climbed a slight incline. We saw many tree stumps. They had been recently chopped down, as the chips were fresh.

Suddenly, an explosion broke the silence. It was quickly followed by a second, as an enemy high-explosive rocket-propelled grenade slammed into something solid. AK-47 fire accompanied the second boom. I heard M-16 fire and frags being returned. The sound was deafening. Moments later, our column turned on itself, as the point element ran back down the trail. In an orderly fashion, we all followed the grunt in front of us and retreated to where the trail had veered right. The FO lieutenant stood in the middle, directing troops as he formed a loose circle. Frenchy's gun was last to enter in the circle so we, of course, faced directly up the trail. If a counterattack occurred, it would be on our gun. I quickly wiggled out of my ruck and placed it in front of our position for cover. I unhooked my ammo boxes and linked up with Frenchy's gun. We were behind a tree trunk, approximately one foot in diameter. We waited for the counterattack. It did not come.

Miraculously, only one soldier had been wounded. He had taken an AK-47 round to the upper left shoulder, but would survive. The FO lieutenant ordered up some firepower, directing it where he thought the enemy basecamp was. The artillery strikes were massive, as the lieutenant walked the incoming firepower all around. A dustoff ship arrived in minutes, and the artillery strikes ceased momentarily. With its highly visible red crosses, the dustoff ship hovered at treetop level while the wounded grunt was extracted on a jungle penetrator lowered with a steel cable. When it had skyed up, the artillery rounds started up again, exploding to our front, approximately 200 metres from our position. Some of the rounds sounded larger than usual. Word spread around the perimeter that the Navy was firing huge guns from ships in our support.

The grunts were hyped up, as we knew we would soon counterattack. My mouth got very dry. Frenchy and I alternated sipping water and drinking cigarette smoke while we strained our eyeballs, looking for movement. Soon, the co's platoon linked up and re-enforced our perimeter. Our platoon was ordered to move toward the enemy, this time about fifty metres to the right of the first ambushed trail. Frenchy and I figured that the gooks prematurely blew the first ambush. They had not allowed enough GIs in their kill zone before firing. We hoped they didn't learn from their mistake. We moved forward in the standard column formation for approximately 100 metres. The vegetation had been shredded from the massive gun strikes as trees were strewn about, splintered and down. The FO lieutenant had come with us to direct more strikes, if needed. We were ordered to form a skirmish line. Frenchy's gun was at the extreme right flank of the line. We moved out slowly on line, hunched forward and low.

All hell broke loose again, as the *clack, clack, clack* of AK-47s opened up. The grunts proned out instantly and returned fire. I could not see the enemy or their bunkers. As I fed ammo, Frenchy delivered his projectiles low, in bursts, spraying left and right. Then, his machine gun misfired. He yelled, "Fire your sixteen." I flipped my selector switch to semi-auto and squeezed off rounds. I still did not trust the auto position. I kept my rounds low, knowing that most grunts shoot too high. I went through two magazines, and was on my third when I heard,

"Cease fire." The FO lieutenant was standing straight up, mid line, holding his .45 handgun, waving for us to fall back. He wanted to direct more strikes. This time it would be airstrikes. We quickly established a perimeter. Frenchy cleared his gun and was back in business.

The lieutenant popped a smoke grenade for visual reference and gave a direction and distance from smoke to enemy. Soon, we could hear and see the spotter plane overhead. The pilot dove toward our position and fired a marker round to our front. Frenchy and I were completely startled as the first fast-moving jet was on top of us from our rear at what seemed like treetop level. The jungle shuddered as the jet roared by and dropped its load on target. I swear we could feel the heat from the exhaust on our faces. The explosions that followed were massive. We could hear secondary shrapnel falling and trees cracking, and feel the heat from the airstrikes. Several runs were made, and there were many explosions.

We fell back another fifty metres to set up our NDP, as darkness was approaching. We would assault again in the morning. All the platoons linked up to form a large defensive circle, about fifty metres in diameter, for the night and sort of surrounded a clearing that had been created by exploding artillery. Doc made his rounds to see if his grunts were okay. Amazingly, no one had been hurt in the second firefight. Claymores were set out and we settled in for a restless night.

Around midnight, we heard a tall tree cracking, then a loud whooshing as it came down. It landed with a thud, directly across a grunt's chest. We knew he was hurt bad, as we could hear him moan through most of the night. All three of the platoon medics attended to him. About an hour later, Doc moved from position to position with an update on his condition. Doc told the captain, "He's got serious internal injuries. We can't help him here." The captain refused the medic's pleas for a dustoff ship, explaining that it was not tactically sound. The hurt grunt died just before dawn.

Dunne was sufferin' big-time. Doc checked him out, and found that he had a super-high fever. It was probably malaria. Our platoon got on line and moved forward. This time, no shots were fired.

Before I knew it, and without realizing what I'd done, I was standing on top of a bunker. The bunkers were almost undetectable, even from just a few feet away. They were set up in a sort of arc, approximately ten metres apart, but kind of offset from each other. It was a major well-established basecamp, not newly constructed.

We established a perimeter just outside the base-camp to dustoff Dunne and the dead grunt. Doc and I strapped Dunne and the deceased to the jungle pene-trator, along with their rucks and weapons. With trees rippling and debris blowing in our faces from the rotor wash, we watched as they rose to the open doorway of the dustoff ship. Dunne had to hug the dead grunt in order to keep his upper body in line with the direction of travel.

Back at the basecamp, I saw huge craters created by the bombing. Right smack in the middle of one crater, I saw human excrement. The turd was dropped perfectly centred and gave proof that the enemy had not abandoned their basecamp until after enduring all that superior American firepower. We didn't find enemy bodies or blood trails. I believe the enemy soldier who had left his mark was trying to make a statement. All your firepower doesn't mean shit. We will endure it for as long as it takes to reunify our nation. Fuck you, GI.

The CO, anxious for promotion, called in a false body count. He claimed that we had killed three enemy soldiers. The Battalion Commander, apparently, was suspicious of the claimed body count, and radioed back that he would be coming in to count bodies for himself. The panicked CO had grunts from the platoon with which he travelled quickly dig some graves. The grunts got creative and put fabrics into the ground so they slightly stuck out, and they actually spread around steak sauce to simulate blood. I could not believe what I was seeing. The Battalion Commander arrived, as threatened, impeccably decked out in custom-fit freshly starched jungle fatigues, with all the authorized patches and rank insignia; highly polished jungle boots; and leather holster for his .45 handgun. He didn't buy the false graves for a second. He relieved the CO of his command on the spot.

We heard huge firefights in the distance. Charlie Company Rangers had been lying in ambush on possible enemy escape routes. Apparently, a large group of enemy soldiers, heavily loaded with gear, walked into GI kill zones. Charlie Company Rangers claimed thirteen dead gooks, and a great deal of seized equipment.

Our company spent the rest of the day carefully poking around the basecamp, always fearful of booby traps. The fleeing enemy had taken everything of value with them. I did see empty cooking oil containers and empty rice bags, all of which had been donated by Americans to the people of the Republic of Vietnam. The food rations were intended for the South Vietnamese, but they had turned them over to the hungry Vietcong. It was impossible to tell who was who unless they fired at us.

* * *

The latest rumour had it that the Division would be withdrawn in March 1970, and that grunts who had more than nine months in-country would be going home. Those like myself who had fewer than nine months in-country would be redeployed to other war zones. Unfortunately, that rumour turned out to be true. Though they didn't let us know until the day of the

Division's "victory" party where we'd each be going, we all knew that we'd probably be sent to a much hotter war zone.

Bravo Company Rangers were now on the move to the rear for final processing. The company linked up at a blueline, just outside a firebase. A perimeter was set up. Groups of three grunts bathed with soap, and then were given clean fatigues. We would be clean for our victory march. Just like in old World War II movies, we humped down the highway to the rear area. It took half a day. We kept a quick pace and were well spaced out with separate columns on either side of the roadway, with our weapons pointed to our outside flanks. We were on display. The highway was busy with traffic, but nobody paid any attention to us. There were no smiling, waving, grateful civilians anywhere.

I was truly happy for the guys going home and envied them immensely. We later heard stories that the entire First Infantry Division participated in a victory march in New York City. Many of the march participants were actually soldiers from other divisions, due to go home anyway, who were temporarily assigned to the Division to bolster the numbers, and to lead Americans to believe a withdrawal was actually taking place.

We cleaned our sixteens and turned them in to Armors. All other weapons and explosives were also handed over. Apparently, all the military hardware belonging to the entire division stayed in place. The

ARVNs took possession of the guns when they took over the war zone. The grunts were weaponless and in party mode that last night. The Army trucked in steaks and beer for our victory party. I and others left the following morning for our new units. Many of the grunts in my platoon went to Cambodia with the First Cavalry Division. Dunne and others went to the American Division, which was seeing beaucoup action in the central highlands. I was shipped up north to Eye Corps (1 Corps Tactical Zone), to join the 101st Airborne Division.

We had all heard the stories of what was going on up north in the 101st. I was about to find out that the stories were true.

5. SCREAMING EAGLES

A flying crane delivering an artillery piece to a firebase in I Corps.

travelled to the northern section of South Vietnam by Air Force C-130 aircraft, alone and weaponless, wearing my steelpot and never-polished jungle boots. I felt betrayed by the Army, the First Infantry Division, the U.S. government, and the whole fuckin' world. I had soldiered through six and a half months of misery and had survived only to be redeployed elsewhere. I missed my old platoon, they had become my family. I vowed to remain distant and not befriend another human being. In the First Division, I had admittedly been a reluctant warrior. Now, I wanted out more than ever.

The once proud 101st Airborne Division had been, in the past, a true airborne division, meaning that all soldiers were airborne qualified. They were known as the Screaming Eagles, and they had been famous for their hard-core attitude and guts in battle. In the spring of 1970, it was obvious those days were long gone. I, and most of the division, were not airborne qualified, and had no desire to jump out of a perfectly good airplane.

I disembarked the aircraft at Phu Bai Airfield, but was met by no one. I stood alone as I read a sign that told me, "All incoming personnel move into this tent." There was no one inside the tent, either. There were c-rations on hand, being warmed in large warm-water containers. All the good stuff was gone so I didn't eat anything. I exited through the rear of the tent and was met by another sign. I said to myself, "This division is so hurtin', they don't even have REMFs to direct you around." This sign informed me to wait here for a truck to pick me up. Eventually, that's what happened, and I was delivered to a reception centre.

The vibe there was not good. I saw 101st personnel screaming at replacements to shape up as if they were back in basic training. Down south, things had been laid back, by comparison, and I was now stressin' big-time again. We hung around there for a few days to process into the Division, and get fucked with. Apparently, there were beaucoup guys who felt as betrayed as I did, because there was lots of yelling, and fights broke out between 101st personnel and incoming replacements.

Eventually, we were shipped off to Camp Eagle for five days of in-country training. The vibe there was outrageous as personnel yelled at and messed with us; more fights broke out. Alone and angry, I ditched the first three days of in-country training by simply staying put in the tent we'd been housed in. On the fourth day, a sergeant found me, and chewed me out. I joined in the training. We were given lessons in rappelling; we would not be jumping out of airplanes, but we would be sliding down ropes from helicopters. "Jesus H. Christ," I thought to myself, "I'm a leg, a ground pounder. What the fuck is going on up here?"

A rumour quickly circulated about a platoon that had just been wiped out. They had been surrounded by NVA soldiers who'd then systematically decimated them. Apparently, there were only a handful of survivors. When training ended, I was assigned to Alpha Company First Battalion 506th Infantry (Airmobile), and specifically, as a replacement to that recently devastated platoon.

We travelled north by truck to Camp Evans, passing through the city of Hue. Camp Evans was a fairly large basecamp with lots of big guns, and the battalion headquarters. It was located just off the main route to Quang

Tri and Dong Ha. Beyond the camp was the demilitarized zone and the huge mountains and valleys that were home to the North Vietnamese Army.

I was processed through Battalion Headquarters and found Alpha Company's orderly room, where I checked in. I was issued new fightin' gear and was ordered to pull bunker guard that night. I would be inserted the next morning and link up with my new platoon.

As it turned out, there were four ex-First Division soldiers on the slick with me the next day, one from my old platoon. As we descended, I could see the little knoll we would be landing on. It was sort of a short bump surrounded on all sides by much bigger bumps. I could see three grunts huddled together off to the side of the knoll. The LZ had not been secured, no perimeter had been established. We un-assed the slick, which skyed up immediately. The RTO grunt loudly said, "Follow us." I saw that he had an external speaker hooked to his ruck frame. He had the volume cranked, and loud radio messages filled the air. We ditty-bopped down a trail for a few hundred metres, where we linked up with the platoon, such as it was.

With the four replacements, the platoon had now grown to seventeen grunts. We were greeted by the acting platoon leader who said, "Man, am I glad to see you guys." I took a quick look around at the sloppy perimeter and my fears were confirmed. "We were in a world of hurt," he told us. The acting platoon leader was a Sergeant

E-6, who went by the handle of "Bollweevil." He was also a replacement to this recently devastated platoon. Bollweevil was on his second tour, having served a few years earlier down south in the Mekong Delta. He was unaccustomed to the rigours of humping the unbelievably steep mountain regions we found ourselves operating in. He was also unfamiliar, as were the rest of us, with fighting the hard-core NVA soldiers who occupied the mountains and valleys here. The platoon was completely green. All the soldiers were brand new, and deep in their personal stumbling phase. They looked beat. They were dirty, skinny, rotten, broken human beings.

The acting Platoon Sergeant was a shake 'n' bake E-5, also green as green gets. Steve Collette was his name and I observed that he was a genuine, sincere individual trying to do his best. The platoon RTO continued to have his volume cranked. The noise blasted through his external speaker as if he were partying in downtown Saigon. I asked him to turn the volume down. He snapped back, "Fuck off, I'm the RTO and I know what I'm doin'." Bollweevil said nothing, and the noise continued. I thought to myself, "Oh fuck, we're all gonna die. These guys have given up." I couldn't believe it, we stayed right there without moving. If the NVA were around, they knew exactly where we were and that our shit was weak. The four First Division replacements started to make suggestions to enhance our survival odds. We were mostly ignored. The platoon was miserable, knowing they had little chance of surviving a year under these conditions.

We operated in the foothills just outside Camp Evans and were finding beaucoup trails but, luckily enough, we were not making contact. Bollweevil, anxious to get some, liked to use three-man mini ambushes. I pulled numerous of these mini ambushes with other inexperienced grunts. Often we would be hundreds of metres from the rest of the weak platoon.

Despite the fact that I had now spent seven months in-country, I began to return to the scared shitless aspect of my stumbling phase. Where were all the professional soldiers, the experienced people who could save lives? They were not in this sorry assed battalion. They had, long ago, figured out the situation, and had done everything in their power to avoid the pukin' buzzards and the I Corps region. How could our leaders keep sending these green inexperienced grunts to certain death in the mountains? We continued to hear stories of squads, platoons, and entire companies ceasing to exist.

As we rotated on and off firebases, we often saw stacks of dead GIs awaiting their trip home. Grunts in our weak platoon came and went so fast, I never learned their names. One grunt, who had received a not-so-serious wound in an engagement, got to go home when his parents, who had not been officially notified by the Army of his injury, found out about it in a letter he had sent home. They had been outraged, and had contacted their congressman. Just like that, he was gone. Another grunt in our platoon "accidentally" shot himself in the foot while cleaning his sixteen. I watched as other grunts on the firebase carried him to the medic's bunker. Instead of grimacing in pain, though, he was grinning ear to ear at the easy way out he had found.

Nixon's withdrawal of troops had destroyed any zeal grunts had left for the war. Nobody wanted to be the last grunt to die in Vietnam. To some Americans, it looked like the war was finally winding down, with victory through Vietnamization in sight. Grunts in the disarrayed 101st Airborne Division knew the truth. For us, the war was more real than ever.

Our operations seemed to have no set length. We were inserted into areas, and left there for weeks until the clothing on our backs was literally torn or rotted off. We would hump up huge mountains to remote firebases, where we wouldn't even get a shower. On firebases, the artillery troops and infantry troops did not get along. CS gas fights would break out between the groups, adding to our nightmares. It was hopeless. I knew our luck would eventually run out, and that we would soon meet the NVA up close and personal.

On operations in the mountains our inexperienced platoon couldn't maintain proper tactical procedures. We often suffered heatstroke victims that had to be dusted off. A dustoff ship would be overhead in minutes, extracting our latest heat stroke victim, but also giving away our position to the enemy. Helicopter resupplies occurred as often as every three days. The slicks would hover over our position, kicking out supplies. With all the comings and goings, helicopters were often over-heard on a daily basis, revealing our location to the patient enemy. We were on his turf and he chose when to attack. We were physically drained as the humping in the mountains took its toll. I considered myself to be walking dead, but I had not given up entirely. I really wanted to survive.

We operated off numerous firebases located between Camp Evans and the A Shau Valley, many of the names of which I can't remember. Alpha Company was on one, when about midday an enemy mortar round exploded just outside a fighting position occupied by our company. I happened to be on the other side of the perimeter, and heard the initial blast. No one had been hurt. A platoon leader, nicknamed "Hoss" because of his large size, along with his RTO, walked the few metres to investigate the blast. As they stood looking at the hole created by the mortar round, a second round exploded in the exact same spot, killing both grunts instantly.

That night, at around 2100 hours, I was walking back to my position, when I heard explosions within the perimeter. I dropped instantly and hugged Mother Earth, afraid to move. Guys screamed, "Incoming, incoming," and ran for bunkers. The gooks had the firebase well sighted in, and were walking rounds all around inside the perimeter. I was lying on steel-wire fencing and was afraid it would somehow blow and rip me apart. I started to claw at the hard ground to make a hole. A round exploded thirty feet away. The concussion blew hard on my body and debris landed all over me. Illumination rounds were fired and night turned to day. I heard, "Brown, here. Come here." I lifted my head to see grunts from my platoon waving me in their direction. Their bunker was no more than forty feet away. I ran and joined my comrades as more rounds exploded all around. While inside the bunker, a round exploded on the corner right at the entrance. We felt the blast, but fortunately, not any shards of communist steel.

The attack ended as quickly as it had started. I don't know how many of our guys died in that attack, but I know at least one did. While I was returning to my position, I saw some soldiers carrying a dead artilleryman, a cannon cocker. After that attack, we knew that the enemy mortar teams had their tubes right on target, and could drop a round on us whenever they felt like it. We all braced for a ground attack, which, in the end, did not come.

Around this time, we received a new first lieutenant who was also an ex First Division soldier. He was Ranger qualified, but had never operated with grunts in the bush. Down south, he had been a mortar platoon leader. He was a short, red-haired, freckled southerner whose radio handle was "Shenandoah." Bollweevil hated the officer instantly and referred to him as "Cottonballs."

Also around this time, I became the Platoon RTO, and once again I carried the heavy PRC-25 radio for the Platoon Leader. The first thing I did as Platoon RTO was to get rid of that ridiculous loud speaker the old RTO had carried. I also set about checking out the other three radios in the platoon. The RTOs carrying them were unfamiliar with their operation and simple maintenance. I quickly instructed them on basic radio procedures. I showed them how to change batteries, and how to protect the handsets from the rain with the hard plastic bags used to ship the batteries. I showed the RTOs how to hang the handset close to their ears so as not to miss radio transmissions, which also enabled them to keep the volume low. I demonstrated how an RTO could softly whisper into the handset, so that he could be heard loud and clear, without raising his voice. Soon enough, they caught on, and we at least had radio communication within the platoon.

Each night after setting up our NDP, I would call in our position and preplotted targets for artillery strikes, if they were needed through the night. All grid coordinates were shackled up into code. There were two methods for this shackling process. One was with a plastic wheel that rotated to the correct digit desired, and referred the user to a code word representing that digit. The second was a preprinted code book which gave different codes for each day. New books were issued monthly, so as not to use the same ones too long. Radio frequencies also changed monthly, and I was on top of those changes. I was also always aware of the "dustoff" frequencies, so I could directly request a dustoff ship.

We truly respected the courage of the aircrews. I never heard of a dustoff ship crew refusing to attempt an extraction. They always came in. The lift ships that carried us in and out of landing zones were also crewed by brave men. On one occasion leaving a firebase for Camp Evans, I was odd man out on an overloaded slick bound for the rear. I saw the door gunner speak into his headset. Seconds later, he waved me over. He shuffled down his bench for me, so I could sit adjacent to him and his M-60 machine gun. I looked his way and smiled a "thanks, dude." I couldn't help but notice the exhausted look on his face. He had the proverbial "tombstone eyes"; they were kind of distant and glazed over with tiny pinpointed pupils. His cheeks were sunken, his eyeball sockets were black all around, and he was dirty and unshaven. His hands grasped the two handles of his gun, and his thumbs rested on the butterfly triggers. He had obviously been flying long hours, and was into self-medication to get through the days.

One operation our platoon went on lasted twenty-nine days. We kept receiving aerial resupply, and the higher ups just left us out there till we either made contact or died of disease. Guys were hurtin' with jungle rot, cellulitis, ringworm, immersion foot, and plain old exposure. Most of us were so exhausted, that we just went through the motions; pick 'em up and put 'em down. We were delirious with fatigue and naturally security suffered. Death was almost a welcome change to more of the same deprivation. I was beginning to believe the grunts had *two* powerful enemies: the NVA and the U.S. Army.

I couldn't understand what was going on. Why were they treating us so poorly? Guys had no poncho liners to sleep in, for fuck's sake. We all knew where they were, though, and why they never made it to us. The fuckin' REMFs had 'em all. They decorated their hootches with them, traded them for boom-boom or drugs, and sent them home as war mementos. The poncho liner thing really pissed us off. Some guys actually humped Army woollen blankets because they didn't have poncho liners. The blankets were outrageously heavy when wet, and they never dried out.

New orders came down that any grunt using C-4 explosive to heat c-rations would be swiftly punished. They stopped sending us C-4 explosive altogether, for Christ's sake. Guys were actually dismantling their claymores and using the C-4 from them to heat their rations. Now that made sense. Guys were disgruntled for sure, and not in the mood to take it any more.

Shenandoah liked to place three-man listening posts around the platoon at night as early warning systems. The grunts were sick of the bullshit and refused orders to pull the dreaded suicidal three-man guard detail. Shenandoah threatened court martials. The grunts threatened fragging in return, and meant it. That was the end of the three-man LPs.

The Army had the solution to its morale problem: kill a gook and get a three-day pass to Coco Beach. Now we had righteous incentive to be warriors. If we killed, we were rewarded with time off the line. In my mind, this was the higher ups' way of admitting that their policies were bankrupt. They now had to buy our dedication to duty.

I was losing my nerve and found it more difficult to soldier on, and we had yet to be inserted into the A Shau Valley, where the hard-core NVA made their home. It appeared to me that grunts were fed into the A Shau Valley on a rotational basis, so as to spread out the casualties. We all knew that before the 101st Airborne Division had been inserted into the area, the U.S. Marines and the Army's First Cavalry Division had fought there and taken ludicrous casualties. We had a few guys in the Company that had survived the Hamburger Hill battle. They spoke little of the engagement, and said things like, "War is hell, but combat in the A Shau Valley is a mother fucker." The enemy maintained roads in the A Shau, and much later in the war actually had a fuel pipeline constructed through there. I suppose grunts were inserted into the A Shau to interfere with the enemy's ability to move supplies south, but it was just so costly in grunt lives that it appeared to many of us to be nothing but a trap.

Our platoon was rotated to a firebase, where we pulled perimeter security. The weather turned bitterly cold, and a thick soupy fog descended over the firebase. Alpha Company was stranded there – nothing could get in or out – so we hunkered down and tried to stay warm.

During the day, we would scrounge up the waxy wrappers that mortar rounds were shipped in, and at night we burned them in our bunkers for heat. By morning, our faces were black from the soot and our lungs struggled to take in oxygen, but at least we were warm.

On the previous operation, I had noticed pain on the left side of my body that progressively got worse. I soon developed a limp and could barely walk. At the firebase, my left leg and groin were still aching, so I asked Doc to check me out. He poked and prodded, then found swelling located in my left groin region. Doc pushed firmly on the swelled-up area, and it hurt like hell. He poked around some more under my left arm, neck, and lower jaw.

"You're all infected, dude," he said. "You gotta go to Camp Evans to get cleaned up."

I thought to myself, "Cool, I could use a few days off the line to get cleaned up." The firebase was still socked in, though, and it would be two more days before the fog lifted and I could catch a helicopter to Camp Evans.

It was late afternoon when I un-assed the slick at the battalion helicopter pad at Camp Evans. I barely knew where my Company area was, having only been there once. As I approached the orderly room, the company clerk, John Finley, met me. Finley was from New York City and quite a character.

"I'll check you in tomorrow," he said. "That way you won't have to pull bunker guard tonight and you can party with us."

"Thanks, man," I replied, "I don't think I can walk to the bunker line anyway."

"Yeah, well, you can go to the aid station in the morning," Finley said. "Let's go chow down."

We went up to the battalion mess hall, but I couldn't stomach the chow. I'm sure the food is fine until Army cooks prepare it. Finley showed me to a hootch with a cot, and I stored my fightin' gear and ruck. I gobbled down some John Wayne bars and fruit cocktail to sustain me through the night. I linked up with Finley and a couple other grunts at Finley's hootch. Soon the bowls and dew came out, and we smoked, joked, and listened to AFVN radio till I couldn't take it any more. Those guys were serious dew smokers, and I was out of practice, having not partaken since the First Division victory party down south. Sleep on the Army cot that night was difficult, as I tossed, turned, and had nightmares.

At the aid station the next day, the medics seemed to know exactly what I had, and went to work immediately. The medic that lanced the infected eruption in my left groin region seemed to enjoy inflicting pain. He showed no mercy as he pushed hard, with two hands, all over the region in order to force the toxic ooze out of the now open sore. The hole was plugged with gauze, and I was issued tetracycline. Each day, for a week, I returned for my torture treatments. Each night, I pulled dawn-to-dusk bunker guard, as the U.S. Army felt I could at least do that while I was shamming in the rear. Between the torture treatments, nightly bunker guard duty, and dew sessions with Finley, I was one exhausted and stoned REMF.

Besides getting cleaned up, I did achieve another minor victory, as Finley and I organized a date for my R&R. Grunts, being superstitious by nature, warned each other "Never take an early R&R." Every grunt that did so, came back to get his shit blown away. With an R&R date of 5 June 1970, I would have eight months in-country. With any luck, I was safe.

Finley and I discussed possible destinations; several were open for my dates. Finley listed them off: Australia, Hong Kong, Bangkok, Hawaii – I stopped him at Hawaii. I told him I'd take Hawaii because Nancy could meet me there. Apparently Hawaii was reserved for married personnel only, but Finley was a company clerk who could arrange anything. Army company clerks knew how the systems worked, and it paid to befriend one. Finley organized the paperwork, and my date was set.

I immediately wrote to Nancy informing her of the news, the dates, and the fact that she would receive a copy of my orders. Now, I had to survive two more weeks in the bush, as I was semi-healed up and had to catch the next resupply slick back to link up with my platoon. I returned to humpin' the radio, more paranoid than ever of getting my shit blown away. Luckily, nothing happened. After a little more than a week, Finley sent word to come in on the next slick. He had arranged to get me in five days early, so I could get my shit together for R&R.

*　*　*

I flew out by Air Force plane from Phu Bai airstrip bound for Da Nang, where I would be catching my flight to Hawaii. I filtered through the rear systems, and ended up at a huge U.S. Marine complex that housed Marine and Army personnel in transit. The barracks buildings were connected to each other internally. The complex was massive and I'm sure could have accommodated thousands of troops. The place was crawling with Marines, all decked out in their flower-power camouflaged fatigues. It was not the place to make jarhead jokes, for sure, as the Marines grossly outnumbered the small representation of Army grunts.

I chatted there with one baby-faced eighteen-year-old Marine who told me about his unit and the heavy casualties they took operating in the mountains around Da Nang. I told him that the same thing was happening up where I was, north of Hue. He nodded in agreement, saying "There it is" and "Don't mean nothin'." He had to return to his unit that day, so we shook hands and wished each other good luck.

By bus, I found my way to Freedom Hill where the Marines had a huge beer garden and even a walk-in theatre with real moviehouse seats. My mission, though, was to locate the PX. There I purchased really tacky civilian clothes and a suitcase for my R&R.

When I returned to the barrack complex, I learned from some Marines about the cool in-country beach R&R centres operated by the Army. I still had three days before my flight to Hawaii, so I got myself on the proper bus, and headed for the beach. The contrast of my life in the bush as a grunt and the beautiful white sand beaches before me was mind-boggling. I walked the beach and saw lifeguard towers, volleyball nets, lawn chairs, barbecue pits, and surfboards. I took a closer look at the waves and watched as they broke, then reformed, then broke again, then reformed again, and then broke one last time. The surf was four to five foot, and very rideable. I asked a lifeguard about the surfboards and he told me, "Yeah, you can use 'em. Just sign one out at the equipment counter." I was blown away. Here I was goin' surfin' in Vietnam on Army surfboards. I quickly changed into my tacky swim trunks, grabbed a nine-foot-six *Surfboards Hawaii*, and charged into the water.

I had been surfing since I was twelve, and, although not of professional ability, I surfed competently and enjoyed it immensely. Surfing had always been more than just a sport to me, it was a lifestyle. Waves in Vietnam were weird with the double reform thing happening, but I soon had it dialled in. I was getting long exciting rides and having more fun than I had experienced in a very long time. I stayed in the water for six hours straight, reluctant to have my fun end. Eventually I had to get out of the water so I wouldn't miss my shuttle bus. As I turned in my board, the lifeguard approached me.

"Dude, nice session, where ya from?"

"Yeah, I grew up in California and have been surfin' for years," I answered.

He was from the Midwest and had just started to surf in Vietnam. He asked if I would be back the next day and if I would go surfin' with him. I told him I would be back the next two days, before going on R&R. I returned to the huge, noisy Marine barracks for the night, and I got up early in the morning to catch the first bus back to the beach. I was on surfari for sure, as I checked out my favourite board and got back to some serious surfin'. The lifeguard dude was on duty, but he managed to get in the water on a break. I gave him some valid surfin' advice, and he caught on quickly; the smile on his face proved it. At the end of the day, the lifeguard said, "Just stay here, dude, I'll hide you out and we can surf tomorrow." Sounded good to me. That night, I stayed in an R&R centre, sleeping in a luxurious bed, and eating food like I hadn't tasted since back home.

I surfed again the following morning, but I had to return to the barracks early to get my stuff together for my flight to Hawaii. I made a mental note to hang around Da Nang for a few days when I got back from Hawaii, so I could surf some more of those weird Vietnam waves.

Nancy was among the wives waiting at the airport to meet their husbands. We were not married, of course, but my clerk bud, Finley, had sent her orders stating we were. We made eye contact, then ran into each other's arms, linking up big-time. Nancy was laughing and crying at the same time, it was a golden moment. We could not keep our hands off each other. The Army had accommodations we could use, but I wanted to get as far away from anything Army as possible. I spent the big bucks and got a room at the Outrigger Hotel right on Waikiki Beach. The luxury of white clean sheets, running water, and flushing toilets was so foreign to me that I had to concentrate, almost force myself to readjust to modern-day life. I was unaccustomed to traffic noise, clanging dishes, television, and not being on guard at night. The colours were blinding, as I had become used to seeing only green. I was like a fish out of water. I felt very alienated, and kind of embarrassed and uncomfortable among the hordes of tourists. Nancy was warm and loving in a way that helped me chill out and adjust to my new, completely alien surroundings.

Nancy and I did all the tourist stuff. We dined, drank, danced, bicycled, swam, sunbathed, loved, and toured around in a rented vw dune buggy. We rented a surfboard and I would push Nancy into the small fun waves in front of the hotel. Nancy giggled like a schoolgirl as she stood up on a surfboard for the first time. I telephoned my folks in California and chatted for hours. They wanted to know how I was, and whether I was in danger all the time in Vietnam. I played down the plight of being a grunt, telling them, "It's okay, it's really not that bad."

Privately, I was stressin' big-time about going back, and actually thought seriously about desertion and hiding out. With my short hair, I would've been obvious at the airport, and arrested immediately by the MPs. With no friends in Hawaii, it would have been difficult to disappear. I had to go back. I could not help but notice all the fat, pasty American couples wearing matching flower-print shirts. I wanted to shout at them, "My buddies are dying in the mud, how can you let this happen? How can you have fun when grunts are suffering?" Nancy could not help but notice the jungle rot scabs on my now healing arms and legs. She also noticed the scarring from my long ago infected hip, and the recent scar from the infected gland in my left groin. She thought I had been wounded. She was also concerned about my weight, as I was down from 150 pounds to a fighting weight of 120 pounds. I told her the weight loss was due to the heat in Vietnam. I assured her I had not been wounded, and that the scars were only from minor skin infections. Five days passed much too quickly, and soon it was time to return to the war. Nancy and I held each other tight, hoping that if we didn't let go, then I wouldn't have to go back. At the airport, we held our embrace until the last seconds of my final boarding call.

On the flight back, I struggled with my sense of confusion and outrage at a society that partied on while grunts died and suffered. I just couldn't understand it. I made a promise to myself to go AWOL in Da Nang, and surf for a week. I ended up back at the Marine transit barracks, and caught the first bus for the beach the following morning.

On the beach, I met some soldiers from a little-known mechanized Army unit that was operating farther north than the 101st Airborne Division. The small isolated unit was known as the "Fifth Mech." It was an armoured outfit, operating tanks and other armoured vehicles. The mech guys told me about the horrendous action they were seeing around Dong Ha, and at the DMZ. I knew they spoke the truth; I could see it in their eyes.

The mech guys were equipped with plenty of dew and a white powdered substance they called skag. I had never seen heroin before and was immediately apprehensive about hangin' out with my new buds. They would just tap a little skag out on a Zippo lighter and snort it up a nostril. One time, they mixed some of the smack in with dew, and lit up a bowl. I inhaled the combination of medications and was real mellow, very quickly. It certainly was not an undesirable sensation and when the pipe came back my way, I inhaled more medicine.

The Fifth Mech guys were en route back to the DMZ from R&R and were hangin' out, reluctant to return to the heavy combat that awaited them. We all hitched a ride up the beach to an Army replacement battalion where they were hangin' out and crashing at night. I liked the location better than I did the Marine barracks so I started hangin' there. I didn't bother registering at the front desk and just sort of kept a low profile and changed barracks nightly so as not to draw attention to myself. During the day, I would hitch a ride back down to the R&R centre to surf all day, then return late afternoon to mellow out with the Fifth Mech guys. They had been AWOL for over a week and were worried about getting busted. When they eventually departed for their section of the war, I hugged each one and wished them good luck. One guy handed me a small bag of dew treated with skag and said, "Stay high and keep low, my brother."

I was still not ready to go back, and I vowed to stay AWOL and surf till I could surf no more. I bought a fine ivory pipe at a local trinket shop and would occasionally smoke a little of the treated dew for medicinal purposes. I linked up with the lifeguard dude and surfed till my arms ached from paddling. He asked me about grunt life, but he was completely unable to relate to the experience. Naturally, his lifeguard tour in no way resembled mine, as he hadn't seen the slightest bit of action. I would later come to the realization that millions of young American men would rotate through Vietnam and never be affected by combat. Actual combat was mostly reserved for grunts, helicopter air crews, firebase artillerymen, and occasionally REMFs, when the enemy launched attacks on rear areas. At this late date in the war, drafted grunts were doing most of the dying.

The lifeguard dude felt a lot of empathy for my situation, and came up with an idea.

"Man, with your waterman skills, you could finish your tour right here as a lifeguard. I'm gonna talk to my captain."

My morale soared at the thought of finishing my tour as a surfin' lifeguard at the cushy R&R centre. He set up an appointment with the commander of the R&R centre for later that afternoon. In preparation for my interview, I showered, shaved, and handwashed my sweat-soaked fatigues. I made sure to put on my fatigue shirt that sported, among many other authorized patches, the Combat Infantryman Badge. I refused, however, to polish my faded, now mostly brown, jungle boots. The never polished boot thing was a line grunt's way of stating, "This is where I draw the line. You can send me into nasty combat situations, but I refuse to polish my war boots."

I knocked on the captain's door and entered, stepping smartly to the front of his desk. I snapped a respectful salute.

"Spec 4 Brown reports, sir."

"Stand at ease for Christ's sake, soldier," the captain said.

The vibe was relaxed as we talked about my surfing and my status in a line company up north. He told me that he thought I would make a dandy lifeguard, but as a line company grunt, it was impossible to get transferred. Once the Army got a soldier as far as a line company, there weren't many ways to get him off. He said, "I'm really sorry, I can't help you." He was a special services specialist and wore no Combat Infantryman Badge. I thanked him for his time, anyway.

Despite the fact that I now knew my return to the bush was inevitable, I continued my defiant AWOL status, surfing daily and self-medicating. Lifer types at my nightly crash site were noticing my presence, so my operations became more clandestine. I even slept alone on the beach, so as not to draw any attention. I was becoming greedy, wanting to stay off the line as long as possible. After nine days of being AWOL, an enlisted lifer type at the replacement centre approached me. He was fully aware that many grunts were hiding out to avoid returning to their line companies, and he was sympathetic. He asked me what unit I was with.

"First Battalion 506 Infantry," I replied.

"Oh yeah, of Hamburger Hill fame." He smiled and said, "It's pretty rough up there in and around the A Shau Valley, huh?"

"Yeah, the battalion is still losin' beaucoup grunts up there."

"Yeah, I know," he said. "We get all the recent rumours, but you know you gotta go back. Tell ya what, you hang around till tomorrow morning, then catch the first flight to Phu Bai and I'll forget I ever saw you."

"That's more than fair, Sarge," I replied. "Thanks much."

He wished me good luck, and I noticed his Combat Infantryman Badge proudly displayed over his left breast pocket.

The party was over big-time, as I checked in at Alpha Company's orderly room. Finley was there, grinnin' ear to ear, and Top, the First Sergeant, was there also. Top was an older soldier, no doubt counting the days till retirement.

"Where ya been, Brown?" he asked.

"Couldn't catch a flight out of Da Nang, Top," I quickly replied.

That was it – no court martial, no Article 15, no nothin'. It was a classic us versus them mini confrontation and I had achieved a mini victory.

Top assigned me to bunker guard that night, and added, "Catch the first slick out tomorrow."

* * *

Alpha Company was on Kathryn, a remote firebase, pulling security. We were preparing to be reinserted, in platoon-size elements, headed in three different directions. I resumed my RTO duties and saddled up. The platoon was bigger and stronger than when I had left. I hated humpin' off firebases, it always felt like we were going in the wrong direction. With all that American firepower aimed at your back, accidents and friendly fire incidents could easily happen, and sometimes did. Also, the downhill grade off of those remote firebases was often steep. Occasionally a grunt would tumble in a klunking heap of man and material.

Out on operation, we found beaucoup trails. Old, new, paralleling, hot, cold – they were everywhere. There was little doubt in our minds that the NVA was all around. Those trails were used by both sides in and around the base of the mountains and valleys. We were not, however, making contact.

Early one morning, about 0200 hours, we were ordered to saddle up and climb to a firebase that had detected movement all around. The hump was virtually double-time, and lasted several hours. The pointman, Martinez, just hauled ass, and the platoon scrambled to keep up with him in the dark. It was a tiny firebase perched like an eagle's nest atop a peak surrounded by many other high peaks and ridgelines. We were quickly directed to fighting positions and poised at 100 per cent alert. In the end, no mortar or human wave assault occurred.

At times, the small firebase was completely socked in during our two-night stay there. At other times daring air crews would land on it and take off. There had been a lot of big-time movement all around the firebase. It was obvious that the full-time occupants were completely spooked. They spoke of regular enemy probings. One helicopter landed and we heard the turbine engine shut down. The crew clamoured around their craft, counting the small-arms bullet holes. There were many. The aircraft was deemed disabled, and sling-lifted to the rear by another helicopter.

Charlie Company of our battalion was securing the small perimeter of the firebase, and Alpha re-enforced during the early hours of the morning. Bunker-line scuttlebutt began to spread concerning the reputation of Charlie Company's commanding officer. Captain Mark Smith, who was also known as Zippo, had reputedly come to Vietnam six years earlier as a private, had never left Vietnam since his arrival, spoke fluent Vietnamese, and had been field grade promoted up through the enlisted and officer ranks. All the grunts were in awe of his experience and many tried to transfer to his company. The grunts in Charlie Company were aggressive and trusted their company commander. In the early seventies, after my tour, I watched TV coverage of initial prisoner releases. One prisoner caught my eye. Sure as shootin', there he was, Zippo was finally coming home. Many years later, I would read more about Zippo in a book entitled *Kiss the Boys Goodbye*, by Monika Jensen-Stevenson and William Stevenson. The book delves into efforts, both private and government-backed, to locate and free American POWs. Zippo's name comes up often.

Eventually, we humped off that firebase to find the enemy, who we all knew was out there. The low vegetation, at grunt height, was gnarly, brambly, twisted, tough thick stuff that you couldn't hack through with a machete. Instead, we used the high-speed trails that grunts and NVA alike used. It was pretty well the only way to move the distances we were required to travel.

Our point team consisted of two Puerto Rican soldiers, Martinez and Ramirez, who only spoke Spanish, and pretty much kept to themselves. There was no rotational thing happening, on point, in this platoon. Martinez and Ramirez were our permanent point team. Sergeant Steve Collette was the permanent point squad NCO. Bollweevil brought up our rear as the platoon sergeant. Shenandoah, the platoon leader, humped mid platoon. As his RTO, I humped directly behind him. I always kept a good interval and only approached Shenandoah if he needed to speak into the handset. Tensions were peaking between Shenandoah and

Bollweevil, who still referred to the lieutenant as Cottonballs. We humped unbelievably steep mountains, the exertion alone took most of our attention. We made no contact, and found ourselves back on Kathryn pulling security again.

We sustained heavy mortar fire on Kathryn, and several artillerymen were seriously wounded. Shenandoah was slightly wounded when a small chunk of shrapnel tore the flesh on the top of his skull. The following afternoon, we were treated to a show, as we stood and cheered an arc light B-52 air strike to the ridgeline suspected of housing the enemy mortar teams. The skies were clear blue, which allowed us to see the B-52 specks at eight miles high. The entire ridgeline exploded as the massive bombs shook the mountainous region. Alpha Company would hump the ridgeline to assess the bomb damage. We found nothing but huge craters and obliterated vegetation. As the operation ended, we received word that Alpha Company was going to Coco Beach for a three-day stand down.

Zippo's Charlie Company arrived at Camp Evans via truck with their latest kill draped over the left front fender, displayed to all like a prized buck. Zippo was trying to make a point with the higher ups. The dead enemy soldier was Chinese. Zippo was saying, "Here's proof that the Chinese are very involved in this war." Apparently, Zippo took heat for the caper because REMFs and civilians alike saw the catch.

We arrived at Coco Beach by truck for the three-day stand down. Instead of relaxing, I was stressin' again big-time. I had a bad feeling about our future. Sure as hell, word trickled down. We were to be inserted into the A Shau the day after our return from Coco Beach.

* * *

Apparently, large battalion-size offensives were being launched again, taking advantage of the improved weather. Alpha Company would be inserted in the A Shau Valley, company-size, on an abandoned firebase peak. We would then descend to the valley below, in platoon-size elements that would take separate routes. My platoon went in first, on a four-slick assault. We secured a large perimeter while the other two platoons and the command group arrived in two sorties. We were the last platoon to leave the landing zone. Our platoon formed up and moved down a finger-like ridgeline. Within 200 metres, I was startled by the sound of the point machine gun as it opened up. There were several long bursts of fire. No radio message was transmitted to me. I attempted to contact the point element RTO with no results. Word was passed back that the point had found definite movement to its front.

The platoon moved on again slowly, descending down the finger-like ridgeline. It was the path of least resistance, and had obviously been well-travelled by foot.

Within 150 metres, the finger descended sharply, to the left, leading down into a creek bed. To the right, the terrain was flatter. By the time I got to the creek bed, I wondered to myself why the point element had chosen this route. I was standing in the small trickling creek, looking almost straight up at the pointman, who was climbing up the steep ravine, which was muddy and without vegetation. Behind me was the other side of the gorge. This bank was also straight up and muddy. I thought to myself, "Oh shit, the NVA will wait till half the platoon is clinging like cats to the side of the gorge, then spring their bush."

Suddenly, word came from the rear that Bollweevil was down and fired up. I couldn't believe it, because we had heard no shots fired. We were too deep in the gorge, however, for the sound to reach us. Before I knew it, Shenandoah was off like a shot to the rear. I scrambled behind, having no idea of what was going on. As I climbed back up to the finger proper, the rear thump gunner said, "Bollweevil dropped his ruck and poked off on his own to the right flats, he's blown away, man."

Just then, Shenandoah arrived, huffin' and puffin', dragging the body.

"I should get a medal for that," he said.

Shenandoah had dropped his gear, then low-crawled the ten metres to retrieve Bollweevil's body. Shenandoah said to me excitedly, "Get the body back up the finger to that flat section, just past that small clearing we passed through."

Things were happening fast. A poncho came out of a ruck, and then the body was in the poncho. I grabbed the left front corner with my right hand, and I grabbed Bollweevil's ruck with my left. Other grunts carried his weapon, steelpot, and web gear. We started climbing in a clusterfuck of ten grunts. Within metres, I was spent. As I gasped for breath, another grunt grabbed my corner. I looked into the poncho, and saw a small entry wound to the middle of Bollweevil's forehead. The projectile had exited through the back of his head, taking most of the skull with it, exposing all the remaining grey matter. I was angry at myself for having run out of steam, then realized I'd been humpin' all my stuff, Bollweevil's stuff, plus my corner of the poncho, while climbing a steep incline. Still, I vowed to quit smoking someday.

It took us approximately ten minutes to reach the bushy area just past the small clearing. I organized the centre where we placed the body. The other grunts assumed a tight circular perimeter around the body, Doc, and me. Grunts asked me if they should put out their claymores. I told them, "Yes." I don't know what the rest of the platoon was up to, but soon we had an air strike goin' on.

A green grunt with one hour in the bush, who had nicknamed himself Cherry, was directing the air strike.

He was relaying through Alpha's captain, who was in contact with the spotter plane. I monitored the radio chat while Cherry popped smoke and gave a distance and direction to suspected enemy positions. The captain talked Cherry through his first air strike, in a calm reassuring voice, by the numbers. I have no idea where Shenandoah and the rest of the platoon were. Grunts were drifting uphill and linking up with my group as the fast movers shook our world with jet blasts and bombs. We had a bunch of cherries; this was their first day in the bush. Soon the strike was over, and in dangerous dribbles and drabs, the remaining grunts climbed up to our position. The perimeter was expanded. As darkness was rapidly approaching, we set up our NDP. I made a decision that I wouldn't eat as a show of respect to Bollweevil, but my commitment was short-lived. Soon, I was scrambling to chow down some cold c-rations before it got too dark. I slept next to the poncho-covered body.

It felt like just another night in the bush. Zero noise. At first light, I received a radio message: there would be a slick on station to extract the body at 0830 hours. I figured: That's two hours away; I got time to eat, smoke, and arrange my radio so that only the radio would be mounted to my ruck frame. There was no sense carrying all food and water when the time came for me to move into the small clearing to be in visual and radio contact with the inbound slick.

I hashed over Bollweevil's death. Alone, he had explored the flat plateau that was directly across from the far side of the gorge where the point element had climbed. Bollweevil had saved countless lives by snooping into the ambush position of an unknown number of NVA soldiers. From their ambush position to the would-be kill zone, the distance had been twenty metres, max. One single NVA marksman could have devastated the platoon by waiting till just the right moment to fire. I figured Shenandoah and I would have made prime targets; find the middle RTO and the platoon leader will be right in front of him. The flat metal whip antenna bobbing above my left shoulder would have been a good clue. Bollweevil got blown away doin' his job. We lived because he died.

At approximately 0750 hours, I heard an inbound slick. The aircraft commander called our call sign and informed me that he was three minutes out. He requested that we pop smoke. They were forty minutes early, my shit was weak. I scrambled to organize my gear. I slammed on my steelpot, slung my claymore bag, which contained twenty magazines, over my shoulder, and grabbed the unmounted radio with my left hand. I heard Sergeant Steve Collette shout, "Hurry up, Brown, they're here." I glanced up to see Steve exiting our perimeter, and stepping into the small clearing. A few paces behind Steve walked a new cherry whose face I had not seen before. Steve had almost crossed the ten-metre clearing, and the cherry was partway across, as I stepped into the clearing. The ambush exploded in our faces, and I was blown back on my ass. Scrambling, proning, and pivoting, I got my eyes to focus and feed me information. Steve was facedown at the end of the clearing; the cherry was down on his back a few paces to my front left. I selected Auto and fired bursts into the bush above Steve's body, emptying one magazine. I released the empty magazine, and inserted a fresh one.

I low-crawled up to the cherry, who was scrambling to get to his feet. I saw that there were numerous small black holes in his fatigue shirt, but could see no blood. I grabbed him by his shoulders, looked into his eyes, and said, "You'll be all right. Lay back down." I hollered for Doc, but got no response. I tried calling for him again, but still nothing. Hunched over, I ran for the perimeter shouting, "I'm comin' in, don't fire me up." I scrambled to Doc's position. I found him there with his tearful face buried in his ruck. I said, "Doc, come on, we got wounded." He got to his feet, and together, we ran back to the cherry's position. He was calm and conscious, and Doc went to work. My thump gunner friend walked over to our position and said, "Steve's done for." He and other grunts had come to our aid, and secured the clearing just beyond Steve's body. The slick must have skyed up at the time of the ambush. I requested a dustoff. An instant radio reply informed me that a dustoff would be overhead in minutes, and that extraction would be by cabled litter basket. I helped Doc tape on plastic gauze wrappers to the cherry's sucking chest wounds. Blood was now visible. Four grunts carried the cherry to the basket, and Doc and I strapped him in. I hollered into my handset and gave the thumb's up. The litter lifted off slowly, then started to spin. The spinning increased dramatically to a rate that was obviously out of control. I couldn't believe what I was seeing, and I thought to myself, "If the holes in his chest don't get him, the spinning will." Later I would hear that he died aboard the dustoff. I had lied to him telling him he'd be okay.

I walked over to the perimeter and asked the thump gunner if he minded if I borrowed his gun for a minute. We exchanged weapons. I launched high explosive rounds in the direction I sensed the ambush perpetrator or perpetrators had fled. I walked rounds all around the hillside while Shenandoah ordered up some artillery. It was all a wasted effort. He or they were long gone. There was no doubt in my mind that the cherry's chest had stopped the rounds that would have been for me. He was directly in front of me when the enemy had blown their bush. I could feel whizzing projectiles all around me. The early arrival of the first slick had thrown Steve and others off. We now had two bodies to hump, as the decision was made by higher ups to link up company-size on the valley floor.

* * *

The platoon moved out, climbing unmolested up the kill zone gorge and descending toward the valley floor. The A Shau Valley was the spookiest, most deadly place I could imagine, and yet, as the sun reached through the tall tree leaves, casting a pretty yellowish colour, its beauty struck me. Just about that time, it was my turn to cross the trail we had encountered. I had never seen a trail in Vietnam like the one I was looking at. It resembled a bush logging road and was plenty wide to accommodate trucks. I observed no truck tracks but did notice boot and sandal prints made by soldiers on both sides of the conflict. I detected a middle hump flanked by depressions, made by tired vehicular traffic. I sensed my Vietnam travels were complete. We were at the enemy's front door, knocking to see if they would like to come out and play. I was zoned to the max with the knowledge that training was over, we'd arrived at the war.

The company link-up occurred successfully and a defensive perimeter was set up, though I had a hard time getting a mental picture of it. Shenandoah and other grunts had gone to powwow with Captain Nicols, our well-spoken company commander. They had taken our dead with them. I thought to myself that there had to be a LZ close by, but didn't know for sure. Doc and I busied ourselves arranging gear. We were the only soldiers in the centre command position of our perimeter. My thump gun friend approached and said, "Brown, come quick; I got a gook." I had heard no shot, so I looked at him like he was fuckin' with me. "I shot him right between the eyes," he said, "but the round hadn't armed and just bounced off his forehead." An M-79 high-explosive round needed to travel a factory-set distance to accomplish enough spins to detonate. The gook had been closer than that distance. As I left my position, I saw a small clearing. The downed NVA soldier was no more than twenty-five metres from where Doc and I sat, chatted, and smoked. As I approached the facedown, outstretched body, I noticed that the thump gunner and three other grunts had taken up walking positions right behind me. It was sort of a V-shape on line, with me at the apex.

It was show time. I was the senior grunt in the platoon, and I had backup. I didn't hunch over, as I slowly approached the gook. My eyes scanned everywhere, though they tended to zero in on the downed NVA soldier. I saw the unexploded M-79 round next to the body. Without moving my eyes, I pointed to the round so everybody knew where it was. One kick could cause it to explode. I really hoped someone behind me was looking periodically at the tree line. I felt ambushed and booby trapped all at once. My selector had long ago been on auto, and my finger wrapped the trigger tight. I was just about to muzzle him in the ribs with my sixteen when he made his move. He rolled away from me, hands immediately extended high above his head, and said something in Vietnamese. It was an unmistakable surrender. We had us a real live NVA prisoner. He was somewhat damaged, what with the perfectly shaped M-79 round indentation clearly visible just above and right between his eyes, but otherwise, he appeared healthy. He sported a neatly trimmed military haircut, an official NVA green combat shirt, and green shorts resembling North American style boxers. He possessed no shoes, hat, ruck, weapon, fightin' gear, or identification. He was, I believe, executing a risky, well-thought out plan to desert his unit, and "chieu hoi," surrender. He appeared to be clean and well fed, but was clearly frightened. I motioned for him to get up, and with the barrel of my sixteen, directed him to move.

We linked up at Doc's location and I motioned for the prisoner to squat down. He was in tears, unable to speculate how many more breaths he would get. Word spread quickly that Martinez had killed an NVA soldier, firing him up with his sixteen. Shenandoah and the rest of the platoon linked up with my element, and I radioed Alpha CP we had a POW to be extracted. We were ordered to link up, company-size, to transfer our POW for extraction. En route, I saw Martinez presiding over his kill like a proud hunter. I also noticed that the live POW humping directly in front of me had a through and through M-16 bullet hole to his right mid-thigh. I made a note to myself to get my ears checked. I couldn't hear small-arms fire any more.

We had arrived for linkup when a group of grunts approached my position to accomplish the POW transfer. The leader of this group was a large, loud, acting platoon sergeant who wanted to shoot our POW on the spot. I quietly countered that he could be more useful alive, but I didn't want to push too hard, so as not to get shot myself. The soldier chilled out, but roughed up our POW anyway. I watched the prisoner as he humped off with his new captors. He glanced back in my direction, and we made eye contact.

Our platoon moved out, and set up our NDP. We did not make contact that night, but we had movement all around us. I fully believed that we'd be overrun, guaranteeing ourselves mention in official Army after-action reports. It was scary. Fear at that level, whether the danger is real or imagined, is not soon forgotten.

The next few days were spent enlarging the landing zone. Grunts used machetes, C-4 explosives, and even a chain saw dropped to us to knock down huge trees. I could not help but speculate that hundreds of enemy eyes recorded our every move for future reference. The other platoons provided security while our platoon worked on the LZ. Squad-size elements of Alpha Company patrolled all around the LZ, reporting no contact.

I was anxious for extraction, knowing that the enemy would soon strike. He would wait until a platoon or company had weak shit, then he would attack. I had almost ten months in-country and was getting too short for this action. I promised myself that this was my last combat assault. I knew from the bowels of my being that I would prefer jail to another assault into the A Shau Valley. I had no confidence that anybody could or would keep me alive. Now, I would take whatever steps necessary to keep myself alive. I had peaked emotionally and was ready to speak up to get out. I lit into Shenandoah, and anybody that could hear, about the absurdity of our existence. I ranted about our zero life expectancy, our zero pride, and our zero hope. I was out of control and Shenandoah had to stop me – "That's enough, Les Brown, hush up." The scene was intense as I chilled for the time being. I was speaking traitor talk for sure, and knew it.

From the fresh landing zone, we humped in a direction that took us to a huge forested hillside that overlooked a large meandering river. The extraction slicks were en route. We were set up in the standard five-position defensive perimeter with the platoon CP at the centre. The CP consisted of Shenandoah, me, Doc, and Ranger. We were approached by "Cherry," the replacement who had directed the air strike of five days prior. Cherry was stressin' to the max as he said, "That's it for me, I'm re-enlisting right now, I'm outta here." I don't know where he got it, but Cherry was tappin' out skag on his hand and snortin' it right in front of everybody.

He was rushin' with buzz as he ranted, and vowed never to hump the boonies again.

The extraction would be tricky, as we were perched on a steep incline. The lead aircraft commander requested smoke. I popped a purple canister in the place where I thought he should place his nose. The pilot radioed he had the colour purple haze, and I confirmed colours via radio. It was open enough for one slick to hover with the uphill skid just touching the slope as six grunts piled aboard from the uphill side. The CP went out on the second slick. The flight was lengthy, and the A Shau beautiful.

* * *

With typical rotational system thinking, the Army allowed us a few days on the firebase to lick our wounds while we secured the perimeter. Alpha Company was scheduled to rotate back into the same area that we just got out of. I would not go with them. While on the firebase, I read an article in *Stars and Stripes* about non-American citizens in the U.S. military being naturalized in Hawaii during their Vietnam tours. I figured with the time it would take to organize such an event, and to travel to it, I could use up a month of my remaining two. I approached Captain Nicols and requested permission to go to Camp Evans to see about becoming an American citizen in Hawaii. He listened as I told him about my citizenship situation, and my desire to go check out the Hawaii trip. He allowed me to go to Camp Evans. Captain Nicols said he would contact the rear, informing them of my status.

I skyed up on the last slick of the day and disembarked onto the battalion pad back at Camp Evans. It was late so I found a cot for later, figuring I'd report to the orderly room in the morning. I chowed down some c-rations that I still carried in my ruck, and I linked up with Finley and other grunts for the nightly dew sesh. After a few bowls, Finley asked me what I was doing in the rear. I asked, "Didn't you get a message about me comin' in from the CO?" Finley had not, so I explained to him why I was here. Finley promised to get on the land line to division headquarters and check it out the next day. The news was not good. The next batch of new citizens would not go to Hawaii for another six weeks. I couldn't believe my bad timing. I did not check into the orderly room, because I needed some time to think things out and plan my personal offensive.

My conviction to never return to the A Shau Valley was total, as I mulled over my next move. I considered any options I had available to use up my remaining two months without going back to the line. I was ready to go to Army jail if I had to. I laid low for two days in the company area, hidin' out and not reporting for the twice-daily formations, which occurred at 1000 hours and 1500 hours. A buck sergeant REMF, finishing his tour, spotted me.

"Brown, what are you doing here?"

I told him the Hawaii story.

"Finley already checked that out. You be at the next formation, or I'll bust your ass good."

I reported at the 1500 hour formation and naturally got assigned to bunker guard that night. While on guard duty, I thought again about my options. I remembered hearing about a recent Supreme Court decision that had set a precedent for new conscientious objector status guidelines. The court had ruled in favour of a young American who had applied for conscientious objector status based on personal rather than religious conviction. Up to that point, CO status had been almost impossible to obtain, except for certain religious denominations such as the Jehovah's Witnesses. A number of would-be draftees had already taken advantage of the Supreme Court decision. I figured that if I declared CO status, I wouldn't be refusing a battle order, but instead stating that I thought killing was wrong, and refusing to do it. I decided the time was right for me to take my stand.

The next day, I reported to the 1000 formation and was informed that I would have bunker guard that night, and that I was to link up with my company the following morning on a scheduled resupply slick. I left the formation and went straight to the armory hootch and checked my sixteen. I told the armour I was going to the battalion aid station, and that I didn't want to hump my weapon. I never touched an M-16 again.

At the aid station, I told the medics I couldn't hear properly, and explained about not being able to hear small-arms fire. They looked in my ears and cleaned out big gobs of ear stuff that had accumulated over time. One medic said, "Your ears are plugged with shit. It's natural for ears to protect themselves from prolonged loud noises. They'll heal up with time." Today, my hearing is still screwed up from all the damage done.

I reported to the afternoon formation and was again told that I had bunker guard, and that I was to link up with Alpha Company. After the formation, I entered the orderly room. Finley, Top, and the buck sergeant were there.

"What do you want, Brown?" Top asked.

"I've turned in my sixteen. I'm applying for conscientious objector status."

"Brown, you have gotta be kidding."

I looked him straight in the eyes. "Top, I've never been more serious about anything in my life."

What followed was a lot of arguing and yelling between me, Top, and the buck sergeant. I told them about the recent Supreme Court decision, which they seemed to be aware of.

"Finley, you call division headquarters tomorrow and check the legality of this bullshit," Top finally said. "Brown, you still got bunker guard."

"I'm weaponless, Top," I replied.

"I don't give a fuck if you take your sixteen or not," Top screamed out. "You still got bunker guard." It felt weird pulling perimeter guard without my sixteen, but nobody else even noticed. I had made a stand, and now I would have to deal with the consequences.

Finley checked out the legalities of my application with division headquarters at Phu Bai. Apparently, I had not yet broken military laws, but there were structured steps that I would have to take to obtain CO status. I was required to see the battalion commander, the battalion chaplain, and a divisional shrink at Phu Bai. I also had to make a statement, in writing, to substantiate my claim. In addition, the Army required five letters from family members and friends to testify to my passive nature. I now had temporary rear status so I could accomplish these tasks. I went to work on my statement, which I anguished over for days until completed.

Finley got me an appointment at Phu Bai to be interviewed by a shrink. I hitched a ride from Camp Evans to Phu Bai on a deuce-and-a-half to make my appointment. I was stressin' big-time, and had just smoked a bowl with other passengers on the truck, when I was dropped off at the shrink's hootch. The shrink was a young captain, drafted after he finished school, and was doin' his time much like I was. He asked about my story and I explained all the poignant facts. He also asked me to talk about my beliefs, to see if they lent credence to my CO claim. I explained how I had always detested violence, and how I viewed my early religious upbringing in the United Church of Canada as being the basis of my beliefs. I told him that I felt it was wrong to take another's life. The interview lasted approximately fifteen minutes, and was over when the shrink said, "I believe you."

I hitched a ride back to Evans and laid low to see what would develop. Top approached me and said, "Brown, pack your ruck, I'm sending you back out." I could not refuse. The paperwork shuffle was in progress, and I had done all I could do in the rear.

I had to adjust to no longer carrying a weapon, and feeling free to move about without first gathering up all of my fighting gear. I could not help but feel somewhat naked, however, as my M-16 had become almost a part of my personality. I now had to radically change my whole way of living, to accommodate my new status. For the past ten months in-country, I had literally walked point for democracy. During the next sixty days, I would walk point for the peace movement, from within the U.S. Army.

I returned to a firebase – which one I can't remember – to link up with Alpha Company. I was ordered to occupy a fighting position on the perimeter for the time being. Another grunt from Alpha Company had also been ordered to occupy the same fighting hole, so naturally we struck up a grunt to grunt conversation. My new comrade went by the name "J.J." Over the next two months, I would spend a lot of time with him.

J.J. was feisty, Irish, from Queens, New York, and always knew what day was Sunday. He had also been in the First Infantry Division during the first half of his tour. He hated the Army and had gotten into trouble for beating the shit out of a lifer type who was fuckin' with him. J.J. was a grunt, but not the bush humpin' type. He had somehow gotten off the line, and now occupied a kind of limbo status within the Army. I never asked him about it; in the grunt world, it would have gone against the unwritten rules to do so. J.J. had an M-16, so I stayed close to him as we organized our fighting position. He told me, "If we get hit, I'll fire my sixteen, you handle the claymores and throw frags." J.J. went and scrounged up as many frags as he could find, and placed them in a metal ammo box at the bottom of our hole. I figured, better a living hypocrite than a dead conscientious objector. I wanted to maintain the integrity of my CO status, but had to admit to myself that if an enemy ground attack occurred, I would be obligated to blow claymores and throw frags to defend myself and others.

J.J. was a big-time self-medicator and was well stocked with dew and smack. He was an intravenous heroin addict and shot up regularly. We needed each other: J.J. needed a friend who could help him out when he was too high to function, I needed to be close to somebody who had an M-16 and would defend me if needed. At times, J.J. would be on the nod with his works still penetrating a vein, and I would have to wake him, so he could untie and clean himself up. I was surprised to see that J.J. never cooked his smack-and-water mixture. He claimed we were so close to the source, and that the white powder was so pure, that it wasn't necessary to cook the impurities out of the smack.

J.J. and I settled into a routine of splitting guard duty at night, and keeping a low profile during the day. My future was up in the air while the Army figured out what to do with me. After about one week on the firebase, a messenger approached me from the battalion command position. He told me that I was to meet with the battalion chaplain.

The chaplain met me just outside the CP bunker, right at the entrance. The battalion CP was the underground bunker that housed the battalion commander and all of his staff, including numerous RTOs, while he was on the firebase. I could hear the battalion radios in the background. Alpha Company was in contact. I recognized the distinctive voice of Captain Nicols as his message boomed loud and clear. I heard him say to the battalion commander, "They won't go, the whole company is refusing to go." Suddenly the battalion commander came bolting up out of the bunker, clearly angry and upset. "I'll court martial the whole fuckin' company. Imagine that, soldiers refusing to attack." It was quite a scene. The commander prepared to link up with his loach, so he could overfly the action and get Alpha moving again. I would hear the whole story firsthand from my thump gunner friend in a few days' time.

The chaplain was all decked out in starch and polish, and he immediately struck me as an individual in the wrong job slot. He stood with hands on hips, rocking back and forth on his toes, in a cocky military manner. He sported a .45 on his pistol belt, the leather holster was highly polished. The man of God, armed with military hardware, wasted no time in deeming me a malingering chickenshit. I told him about my deeply rooted religious beliefs. He said, "Bullshit, you're no CO." The interview was over, and I returned to the bunker line.

A few days later, J.J. and I were ordered to police the area out in front of the fighting positions, in order to keep the lanes of fire clear. It was always spooky poking around out front, amongst all the claymores, dud grenades, and fugaz barrels. I heard somebody call my name, and looked up to see my platoon humping in through the wire. My old thump gunner friend approached me: "Brown, you would not believe the shit that just went down in the past few days." He went on to explain. The platoon had been humpin' down a finger, when it had walked right into an NVA ambush. The pointman, "Cap," a new replacement grunt, was down and instantly fired up. The NVA did not hit and run but instead maintained a classic L-shaped ambush. Every time a grunt moved even slightly, the enemy opened up with AK-47 fire. The platoon was pinned down big-time and called for a company link-up to assist. Shenandoah ordered a grunt up to recover Cap's body, and he, too, was shot up. After the company arrived, a third grunt was killed attempting to recover the first two bodies. Even after air and artillery strikes, the NVA did not abandon their well-thought-out ambush position. Apparently, this was when the Alpha grunts refused to move into the deadly kill zone. The thump gunner named off the two other grunts besides Cap who had been killed, but I did not want to hear who they were. I simply blocked it out.

The thump gunner dude hadn't finished telling his story. He continued:

"After a while, we could tell they were gone so we got the scene cleaned up and the bodies airlifted out. We moved out from that location, platoon-size, and set up our NDP. We had just got our claymores out, when the lieutenant ordered up some mortar fire. The first round was supposed to be 150 metres outside our perimeter but the mother fucker exploded dead centre in a six-grunt position. Brown, we had to find the pieces and put them in a plastic bag. They were vaporized, blown to rat shit, there was nothing left."

He named off six more of my comrades, killed-in-action, but I mentally blocked out these names as well. I just couldn't absorb any more. I asked if he was sure that a friendly mortar round had blown away the six grunts.

"There is no doubt in my military mind," he said. "I heard by radio that the round was out. Seconds later, it exploded right on top of us. The lieutenant said it was a gook mortar, but we all know it was a GI mortar." He walked off, shaking his head, and said, "Take 'er easy, Brown."

I knew all of the KIA, but to this day, I don't know who died. The guilt I felt for not being there with my comrades, as they got blown away, will haunt me forever.

The next day, J.J. and I were hangin' at our fightin' hole when I heard a group of grunts loudly approaching us from further up the fighting line. It was the captain of Delta Company, accompanied by his RTOs and entourage, comin' to fuck with the CO who occupied a fighting position on his bunker line. The captain, nick-named "Ranger," yelled, "Which one of you is the chick-enshit CO?" I replied, "That would be me." Ranger went on to deride my very being, calling me all types of nasty names. I said nothing in reply, knowing he would soon tire if I didn't bite. Sure enough, he stomped off, satisfied he had done his duty.

Two weeks later, news of Ranger's death and the slaughter of his company would circulate around the bat-talion. Delta had been inserted back into the A Shau Valley in a company-size group. I believe the insertion attempt was made into the LZ that my platoon had cut out just a few weeks before. Apparently, the NVA had been poised all around the LZ with sighted-in mortar tubes and a well-organized plan to do in the next American unit to attempt to return to the area. The enemy allowed the entire company to get on the ground before launching their attack. They viciously mortared Delta Company, and Ranger called for an extraction. The enemy moved in on the company and engaged. Ranger was killed when the slick he was attempting to board took hits and rolled over. The main rotor blade cut him in half. Delta Company had suffered 60 per cent killed or wounded during the battle. The First Battalion 506 Infantry (Airmobile) of the 101st Airborne Division was in a world of hurt. Other battalions were being rotated in and out of the A Shau, also taking heavy casualties.

A few days later, Shenandoah approached me and said, "Come on, Brown, you're with me." Shenandoah had just been assigned to lead the battalion forward supply unit. The forward supply unit (FSU) was responsible for coordinating the supply of grunts in the bush. I was to be the radio operator for his unit. My job would be to operate the radio, communicating with the line companies in the field, and the helicopter crews that flew the supply missions. My new job was one of the most sought-after ones in the battalion. I was off the line.

* * *

I really had no idea what had actually happened behind the scenes to put me in this new, non-combat job. In my

mind, I envisioned a meeting of higher ups, discussing
what to do with me. I had soldiered through ten months
of humping the boonies, narrowly escaping death on
many occasions. I had not refused any orders, and, up
until my recent efforts to get off the line, had generally
been a sound trooper. I speculated that some sort of
agreement was reached to assign me to the FSU, thus
giving me what I wanted, while letting my CO application get lost in the paper shuffle. I would finish my tour.

The FSU consisted of Shenandoah, me, J.J., the Joker,
and Eggrat. On firebases, I'd man the radio, Shenandoah
would bark orders, and the rest of the team would gather
up the required ammo, replacement gear, c-rations,
water, sundry packs – and grunts – bound for the bush.
Slicks would arrive on the landing pad, and we'd all
pitch in to quickly load the bird; they'd be on the ground
for only moments. Some days were so busy we'd have
resupply stacks grouped all over the pad. Other days, we
could chill.

Generally, communications were good and I seldom
had to relay messages through a radio relay team. The
line companies operated mostly within range of the
artillery batteries of the firebase we were working on. We
travelled often, rotating on and off of firebases. Some I
had been on often, some were completely new to me.
Occasionally, when the battalion conducted sweeps
through the foothills between the A Shau and the coast,
we operated out of Camp Evans. We had a hootch there

adjacent to the battalion pad. It was the only hootch I ever had in Vietnam, and the only place I could ever vaguely call home. I still lived out of my rucksack, though. I kept it stocked with c-rations and batteries. We were always ready to saddle up and move our operations at a moment's notice, as the battalion's movement dictated. The radio work was hectic at times, as I tried to keep up with the comings and goings of supplies, grunts, and helicopters. Quite often late at night, I'd be hunkered down with a red-lensed flashlight, copying down lists of supplies required by companies and individual platoons in the bush.

Sometimes units would need an emergency supply of ammo, or whatever, and would not be close to an LZ. We would organize a "kick-out" mission to get the supplies to the grunts. Shenandoah liked to go out on the kick-out missions personally but occasionally would send another FSU team member. My first kick-out mission was a learning experience for sure. The helicopter was loaded with M-16 ammo, c-rations, and water contained in round metal, artillery canisters. We were resupplying an isolated platoon that occupied a thickly vegetated hilltop position. The slick crew chief hollered at me to keep an eye on him for the thumbs-up signal, which would let me know when I should kick out the supplies.

Soon, I felt the slick flair, and I could see the grunts hunkered down on their tiny protruding peak. I got the thumbs-up signal, but thought that we weren't close enough to the grunts so I was reluctant to kick out the stuff. We were at a treetop hover, a very vulnerable position for slick crews. Suddenly, the crew chief abandoned his machine gun and scrambled to the open cargo area. Hunched over, he started throwing stuff out very quickly. I got the idea and, in seconds, we had kicked out everything. I could see the cases land on the steep incline, and then roll downhill away from the grunts. They looked skyward and shook their fists at us. They were going to have to hump down to the supplies, then hump them back up for distribution among the platoon. I could only guess that the aircraft commander had positioned his craft where he thought it would enhance his crew's survival odds. We were in and out in under a minute. I learned that when the crew chief gives the thumbs-up, it is most definitely time to kick out the stuff.

I got to know many of the battalion RTOs through our work, and I would occasionally hang with them on firebases to smoke dew and shoot the bull. All RTOs had been grunts originally. They had carried the platoon radio, then had graduated to company RTOs and finally to battalion RTOs. One battalion RTO I met was Alan Duffy, from Allentown, Pennsylvania. He had been the RTO in my Alpha Company platoon, prior to my arrival there. Duffy had been there when the entire platoon had been wiped out. He told me the chilling story in detail. It was one of the spookiest I would ever hear.

The platoon was scheduled for a resupply, and had located an old, one-slick, GI-cut LZ. They had arrived at the LZ in the morning, but the resupply was scheduled for noon. All the slicks were occupied on large insertions elsewhere, and the resupply kept getting rat-fucked until a slick was available. The platoon stayed in place the entire day waiting for resupply, which finally came just at dusk. All the while, the enemy had been monitoring the platoon.

As Duffy spoke, I could see the enemy watching the platoon with binoculars, sketching each grunt's position, in detail, on paper. Duffy's words were haunting, as he continued the story:

"After the slick skyed up, we just moved back into our daytime positions, passed out the c-rations and water, and set up our claymores. Night had fallen. We should have moved – even fifty metres – but didn't because of the darkness.

"The night was quiet and still. Too quiet. The enemy must have worked all night to sneak up and completely surround us. We never heard movement." Duffy spoke in a soft monotone voice as he relived the experience. He looked straight into my eyes and continued.

"At about four in the morning, all fuckin' hell broke loose. They threw satchel charges, chicom grenades, and homemade explosive devices at us; there was no AK fire at all, man. Guys blew their claymores and opened up with sixteens, thump guns, and machine guns. Soon guys were screaming, 'Don't blow your claymores.' The gooks had located them and turned them around to face the GIs, who were now detonating them, spewing concussion and steel pellets back on themselves. The moaning of the dying and wounded only attracted more explosive devices to that position. Guys were screaming, 'Don't fire your sixteens,' as that also attracted explosives.

"I just laid on my back," Duffy said, "looking up to see sparkling devices coming my way. All I could do was roll away from each one and hope I saw them all coming. Soon, only the delirious moaned and groaned. The gooks threw more charges to silence them. We figured it out: don't blow claymores, don't fire weapons, and don't moan and groan, in the hope they would think we were all dead and go away. It was not a hit-and-run attack. The gooks held their tight circle and systematically delivered the carnage. Then, they were gone."

"Why didn't the gooks overrun your position?" I asked him.

"No need," he replied. "We were fucked. Me and three other guys were the only ones not wasted or badly wounded. I couldn't even radio for help at first, as all the radios had been blown to rat shit. I scrambled around and scrounged up a good handset, an antenna, found a battery, and got a radio working. I called for company link-up. The other platoons in Alpha had heard the firefight and were already en route in the dark. Me and the survivors started treating the wounded. I don't wanna talk about that part. The company linked up just before dawn. Dustoffs came, and it took all day to get first the wounded, and then the dead, out. The whole company was extracted. We went to Camp Evans to reorganize and lick our wounds."

Duffy was awarded the Silver Star for his efforts to regain radio contact and direct rescue efforts. After our tours, Duffy and I were assigned to the same unit at Fort Benning, Georgia. He never spoke of the engagement to me again. Duffy's recounting of our platoon's demise only re-enforced what I had already learned: while helicopter support saved lives, our dependence on it could also greatly contribute to our woes.

On the same firebase, I was approached by the Texan, the crazed grunt from my old platoon in the Ranger Company down south. I didn't recognize him at first. His crazed grunt look had been replaced by the scared shitless grunt look. He had lost weight and was no longer boisterous and gung ho. I had no idea he was in the battalion and was surprised to see him.

"I got thirty-two days and a wake-up, man," he said, "I don't know if I'm gonna make it. We're losin' too many guys. Did ya hear about Daffy?"

Daffy had also been in our old Ranger platoon and was well liked by all the grunts. "No, I didn't know Daffy was up here."

"Yeah, he got his shit blown away the other day," the Texan said. "He was humpin' the lieutenant's radio when he took an AK round to the head. It was a one-shot sniper deal. We never saw the sniper. Daffy had humped the lieutenant's radio so he could get off point. I'm sick of this shit."

"There it is," I said.

"I gotta get over to my hole, man; take 'er easy, Brown."

"You too, man."

His company had just humped up to the firebase and I watched as the grunts assumed their fighting positions. I thought to myself, "Holy shit, look at these green young kids. They've got one long year ahead of them." Fear was written all over them.

* * *

The FSU returned to Camp Evans and was operating from the battalion pad, so we crashed on cots in our hootch. J.J. would make occasional forays to purchase skag, dew, and new works. The drugs he'd buy from kids anywhere and his hypodermic works he'd buy over the counter at a Vietnamese pharmacy in Hue. One day, J.J. came back with his usual goods plus a new item he had bought at his favourite pharmacy. The new item was called "Obesitol," a liquid taken orally for weight reduction. It didn't settle well with J.J. and he was one cranky, pissed off dude.

The Joker and I were hangin' in the hootch when J.J. came bustin' in, cursing about the Alpha Company buck sergeant. Still feeling the effects of the drugs, he had run into the buck sergeant and gotten into a verbal altercation. We all agreed that the sergeant was a lifer asshole. J.J. got even angrier. He grabbed his sixteen and bolted out the door saying, "I'll handle this."

The Joker and I looked at each other and said, "Oh, shit." We had to stop him. We ran to catch up with J.J. just as he was approaching Alpha's orderly room. I got in front of him. "Don't do it, man," I said, "you're too short to go to LBJ."

J.J. pushed me in the chest and said, "You want some of this too?" meaning his M-16.

"No, man," I replied, "we love you too much to let you do this." That got his attention and he semi-chilled out.

"Okay, okay," J.J. said, "but if that mother fuckin' lifer ever fucks with me again, I'll fuckin' waste him." The buck sergeant had seen him coming and from that day on never said another word to J.J., the Joker, or me. Back at the hootch, J.J. tied off, fired up, and fell asleep.

"That was close, dude," the Joker said. "You just know he was gonna do him."

J.J. knew many of the junkies at Camp Evans and there were lots. I had not been exposed to heroin down south but the white powder was readily available up north. Guys were shooting it up, or snorting it, or smoking it with tobacco or dew. Guys who had never seen drugs back home were now addicts. For ten bucks, you could buy a vial as big around as your thumb and about one-and-a-half inches tall, two-thirds full of 96 per cent pure heroin. We all knew somebody was cashing in on the drug trade big-time. Some guys even thought American high-ranking officials were involved; I wouldn't like to believe that, but anything is possible.

* * *

One day I was walking back to the battalion pad, when I rounded the corner of a nearby hootch, and stumbled right into Delta Company. Since the horrible battle of a few weeks prior, Delta had been laying low to lick their wounds and take on replacements. The company was seated on their butts classroom-style in one tight clusterfuck. The devastated company had been restocked with cherries and was getting a pep talk from a colonel. In the moment it took me to walk by, I heard the colonel say, "Sure, we took a tough blow, but we're not going to let that slow us down. We're gonna go right back out there and kick some commie ass." I could not believe what I was hearing. The company was made up of over 60 per cent FNGs who had not had one day in the bush.

I was tempted to shout out, "Don't go, you're all gonna die, you're not ready for the A Shau," then run like heck. It was pathetic. I put my head down, my hands in my pockets, and dragged myself to the pad for the scheduled afternoon resupply sorties.

I was running out of fight and my body was experiencing some kind of shutdown. I had no idea what was wrong with me, but I had zero energy. I felt like rapidly hardening cement, and I ached everywhere. If the rest of my unit were up in the morning talking, I would hear their voices but I would be unable to tune them in or to move my body. I was in some weird zone that I couldn't name, and anxious to get past. I had stopped writing letters home, and medicated often with J.J., Eggrat, and the Joker.

Apparently, word of my CO application had circulated and grunts were finding me to ask how I'd done it. I'd explain to each how I had turned in my sixteen and gone to the orderly room to declare my status. I also explained the steps that I had been required to take. A few grunts asked if I would help write up their declarations and I said, "Sure." Apparently, there was a run on CO applications shortly after mine and the lifers had to do something about it. While working on the pad during resupply hours, I started to see something that really spooked me. Some grunts had turned in their sixteens and were being sent to the bush without a weapon.

Nobody had messed with me about my CO status since the time Ranger had chewed me out just prior to my assignment to the FSU. I personally never heard a word of disapproval from other grunts. Many grunts would say things like, "Way to go, man," as if I had scored a victory for our side. Around this time I was notified that the battalion executive officer wanted to see me. I reported to him at battalion headquarters as ordered where he called me nasty names. I ignored his verbal assault, and played dumb. Eventually, he became frustrated.

"The battalion commander wants to talk to you, Brown."

"Anytime, sir," I said, with just a hint of rebellion in my tone.

"He'll send for you soon. Now get out, Brown."

About a week later, our battalion moved south to Firebase Bastogne, an older firebase nestled into a valley surrounded by rolling foothills. The FSU occupied bunkers at the centre of the firebase adjacent to the battalion CP. The second day there, Shenandoah said that I was to report to the battalion commander that evening at 1900 hrs. It was show time again, as I started stressin' about talking to the head grunt himself. I had several hours before my meeting with the commander, so I went off by myself to mentally prepare for the interview. I promised myself that no matter what happened at the interview, I would hold my ground, and defend my CO position. There was no doubt in my anti-military mind about the depth of my conviction, I just hoped the battalion commander sensed that too.

I reported to the battalion commander in his dimly lit World War II style tent. Behind the large wooden desk where the commander was seated stood the American flag, and the battalion colours and campaign banners. I stepped smartly to the desk, snapped a crisp salute, and said loud and clear, "Spec 4 Brown reports as ordered, sir."

The CO returned the salute and said, "Stand at ease, Brown." I assumed the at-ease position and waited to see what would develop.

"I understand you're applying for CO status, Brown."

"Yes, sir."

"What would you say if I called you a yellow chickenshit?"

"I'm no coward, sir. I've been here over ten months. I've been ambushed, rocketed, mortared, and I've seen more booby-trapped dud rounds than I can remember. I've seen plenty, sir."

"Tell me the basis of your claim."

"Well, since my childhood in Canada, I've always been taught killing is wrong, sir."

"You're Canadian?"

"Yes, sir."

"What the hell are you doing here, Brown?"

"I was drafted, sir."

"You mean you volunteered for the draft and then volunteered for the infantry."

"No, sir, I didn't volunteer for nothin'."

There was a long pause.

"I understand you were in the Big Red One the first half of your tour. What outfit were you with?"

"Bravo Company, Second Battalion, Sixteenth Infantry, sir."

"That's the Ranger Battalion, isn't it?"

"Yes, sir."

"Good outfit, they have a solid reputation."

"Yes, sir."

"I understand you're temporarily assigned to the FSU."

"Yes, sir."

"Tell me about your duties with the FSU."

"I operate the FSU radio, sir."

"Gets pretty hectic some days I bet."

"Yes, sir. Some days are extremely busy."

"How much time left in your tour, Brown?"

"Thirty-eight days, sir."

"Well, Brown, I just wanted to talk to you; I like to know what's going on in my battalion. You can return to the FSU and finish your tour. You're dismissed."

I saluted again, and the battalion commander returned what looked like a respectful salute.

I went back to the FSU bunker where I was met by Shenandoah, J.J., Eggrat, the Joker, Duffy, and Finley, who had linked up on Bastogne because of the battalion movement.

"Well, how'd it go, dude?" Finley asked.

I grinned ear to ear. "You're lookin' at the FSU radio operator for the next thirty-eight days." The ex-grunts slapped me on the back and shook my hand. Even Shenandoah seemed pleased. Then the enlisted trash went outside to smoke numerous bowls to celebrate.

* * *

The battalion was constantly on the move, covering areas in the southern regions of the 101st Airborne Division's area of operations. I suspect the battalions we were covering for were being rotated into the A Shau Valley. The FSU didn't have much to do at this time, because our line companies were pulling rear area security duties. We just hung out together at a bunker or a hootch, awaiting orders for our next move.

One day, we found ourselves way down south on the flatlands helping to provide bridge security. We occupied a hootch to the side of the bridge and a group of ARVNs occupied makeshift hootches across the road. In actuality, the ARVNs were securing the bridge, and we were just hangin'. About 0400 hours, a firefight erupted across the road at the ARVNs' location. It sounded like the Battle of the Bulge as ARVNs opened up with claymores, frags, sixteens, and prolonged machine-gun fire. The FSU team evacuated the hootch and took up bunker positions to see what was up. We saw no enemy soldiers but remained poised till daylight. Eventually, an ARVN lieutenant approached and wanted us to come see. "Beaucoup NVA, Beaucoup NVA, La Dai, La Dai," he said. We all saun-tered across the road and, sure enough, the ARVNs had two enemy soldiers down and fired up in their kill zone.

The Joker had been ordered to get an Army driver's licence, so that he could haul us around to wherever we were needed. The Joker loved his new job and liked to cruise us around in his truck. One day, anxious to take a trip, he pulled us off the main route onto a pathway that led to the beach. In the distance, we could see the white sand, and my nostrils filled with that salty, damp, pungent beach odour. I was stokin' at the prospect of doing some body surfing and hangin' out. As we moved slowly down the pathway my short timer's outlook got the better of me. I imagined NVA ambushes behind every bush by the roadside. It was too spooky for me and I told Joker to stop the truck.

"What's the matter, Les, losin' your nerve?" J.J. asked.

"I'm too short for this bullshit," I said. "You guys go ahead. I'll walk back out to the road."

The guys bickered back and forth and finally decided to put it to a vote. Before we voted, the Joker took the time to tell us about some Marine who had been cruising around in a Jeep in this same area only to be captured by the NVA. (After the war, I would read about the capture of U.S. Marine Bobby Garwood, who would be the subject of a controversial court martial when he returned after fourteen years as a POW.) The Joker's story swayed the vote to three to one against going to the beach. Eggrat still wanted to go. He whined like a snot-nosed kid, but the majority ruled. We backed up right on out of there, and never did see the South China Sea.

The Joker drove us up to a firebase just off the route to Da Nang. The firebase was situated on high ground, and dominated the mountain pass region we were now in. Word spread quickly that a U.S. congressman would be on the firebase for lunch. Apparently, a full-blown congressional investigation was being conducted to see why so many grunts were getting blown away in I Corps. We had never seen a firebase quite like this one. In the centre, there was a huge messhall large enough to seat hundreds of soldiers. The firebase must have been an Army showpiece for visiting dignitaries because it in no way resembled the tiny perched outposts we were used to. We walked into the messhall and could not believe what we saw. KPs were setting long tables with silverware and freshly laundered white tablecloths. We all slapped our knees and burst out laughing. Some lifer spotted us and screamed at us to get the fuck out before the congressman got there. As we left in our three-quarter-ton cruisemobile, we saw fat and happy soldiers, wearing clean new fatigues. They didn't resemble grunts at all.

We laughed hysterically at the sham the congressman was being treated to. We all knew that he would never be allowed to go near the A Shau Valley, where the war really raged.

The higher ups sent the FSU back north to Camp Evans to prepare for the battalion's reinsertion into the A Shau. The line companies were still down south, however, enjoying their respite, so our unit had very little to do. J.J. figured this was a good time to go to Saigon on a three-day mini vacation. He asked Shenandoah, "How 'bout lettin' us have a three-day pass?" never mentioning Saigon.

"I don't care where you guys go," Shenandoah replied. "Just be back in three days cause we'll be running resupply missions again."

I had never seen J.J. so animated as he barked orders to the Joker and me, "Pack your shit, boys, we're goin' to party town."

J.J. had contacts all over Vietnam and knew a black transportation company clerk at Camp Eagle who fabricated phoney travel orders for a price. Shenandoah had given us permission to go, but we needed official orders that showed we were legally en route to Saigon. Before leaving Camp Evans, J.J. prepped us for our meet with the clerk and his cronies. They were all smack freaks, and suspicious of outsiders, so J.J. had to teach us their official handshake greeting so we would be accepted as friendly. I was down to twenty-seven days left in-country, and paranoid about going anywhere, but this time figured what the heck, I could get unlucky here or in Saigon.

At the clerk's hootch at Camp Eagle, we all went through the prearranged handshake greeting with the clerk and his hootch mates. The clerk was a cool dude who sported a full-blown afro and beard, and enough fine Asian gold jewellery to make Sinbad drool. Soon drugs, both hard and soft, appeared and we all grabbed some Zs. The next morning, with the necessary paperwork now in hand, we hitched a ride to the airstrip at Phu Bai and caught the first flight to Saigon via Da Nang.

J.J., who had been to Saigon before, played our tour guide as he masterfully got us from Tan Son Nhut International Airport to downtown Saigon via several different modes of transport, including a Vietnamese taxi. J.J. had insisted we each take our own cab and enjoy the ride. The taxis were sort of open three-wheeled rigs that resembled a North American ice cream bicycle, but powered by noisy, stinky, two-stroke engines. The passenger rode up front on a padded bench seat and became, for all intents and purposes, the front bumper. The psycho drivers, seated at the rear, drove through the busy city with seemingly no regard for life or limb. It was more exciting than an "E" ticket at Disneyland, but also much more hazardous.

The Presidential Hotel, where we were staying, was huge and overrun with partying GIs, drug vendors, and big city boom-boom girls. The shady-looking drug dealers hung out on the front steps at the entrance. Naturally, everything was available. The boom-boom girls hung out at the bar upstairs and would approach each new guest, honk his horn, and then sniff his clothing, for what I don't know. We all partook in everything and crashed for the night. We spent only two nights in Saigon, but I sensed that, with enough cash, absolutely anything, from Howitzers to human beings, could be purchased.

J.J. took his tour guide duties seriously. We had lunch on a restaurant barge docked downtown, which was known for its fine Asian cuisine. We toured the happening Saigon club scene, and ended up in a high-class nightclub that showcased Vietnamese musicians and singers. The club patrons were mostly Vietnamese men and older American gents wearing expensive civilian clothes. The headliner was a beautiful female Vietnamese vocalist who sang in her native tongue. She was wearing an elegant long, black, sleeveless evening gown, with white pearls and long black gloves to match. I couldn't understand the lyrics, but the warmth and beauty of her voice gave me goosebumps.

It was time to go back up north as our time and cash had been depleted. At Camp Evans, it was business as usual, as the FSU resumed its duties. We operated again on the battalion pad, and crashed on cots in the FSU hootch. I fantasized a lot about how absolutely perfect life would be as a civilian. These fantasies and expectations were so elevated in my mind, that I was bound to be disappointed. I, as well as others, I suspect, were unknowingly setting ourselves up for a major letdown.

During his one-year tour of duty, a grunt went through many different transitions and stages. I can almost recall the exact point of each transition for me. I began with my personal stumbling phase and moved into the "somewhat assimilated" phase and then into the "I'm good at this and won't die" phase. At about that time, a grunt has reached the halfway mark in his tour and has to make it through the last six months. In my case, when I was re-deployed to the 101st Airborne, I reverted back to the "scared shitless" initial phase. I then went through a three- to four-month period where I was experienced enough and loose enough to be an effective grunt. The rest of my tour I was too miserable and angry to be effective. I can't speculate on what other grunts' experiences were like, but I can't help believe that mine was fairly standard. There were those who thought a longer tour of duty would have delivered better results. This might be true, but I would only remind those opponents that the one-year tour of duty was how the U.S. government marketed the war to the American people in the first place. Besides, all the grunts I knew were pretty well used up at the end of their tours.

While working on the pad one day, I saw an entire company awaiting slicks to make a combat assault.

I didn't recognize any of the soldiers and asked Shenandoah what company it was.

"That's Alpha," he said. It was my company and I didn't recognize any of the soldiers. Captain Nicols was gone, replaced by the battalion communications officer, who wasn't even a grunt. I guess he would learn on the job like the rest of the grunts or perish trying. My sense of betrayal was complete. The system couldn't even provide competent or experienced company commanders to lead the inexperienced grunts. America was extricating itself from Vietnam and turning its back on those sacrificing their lives. Nothing made sense any more. I would never again trust a government at any level. I hadn't trusted the M-16 issued to me, I didn't trust air and artillery support that blew away grunts, I didn't trust dustoff litter baskets that spun out of control, I didn't trust life itself. I sensed that if I did survive, I would heal someday; I just didn't realize that it would take decades to accept and forgive.

* * *

I was short, so short I could barely control the electrical charges of anticipation that shook my body. The excitement was beyond any I had ever experienced. My war was virtually over. The FSU was operating on a firebase when I received word to return to Camp Evans for final processing out of the battalion. As I shook hands with the FSU team, I could not help but notice the fresh stack of poncho-covered lifeless GIs awaiting their return to the world. All bodies were alive aboard the last slick ride I would take in this man's Army. As I cleared battalion and company paperwork, I was struck by a new fear. Though I couldn't believe it, I was now afraid to go home.

At Phu Bai, I cleared divisional headquarters, where the clerks treated us grunts with disrespect. It was late so I had to spend one more night at the same reception centre I had stayed at upon my arrival in the 101st Airborne Division. I found a cot, chowed down, and when it got dark, went to watch the nightly Vietnamese band entertain the troops. As the band belted out John Fogerty's "Proud Mary," I chuckled as the lead singer, unable to pronounce his Rs, chanted, "Wollin', wollin', wollin' on the wiver." There was a substantial audience assembled. Most watched the two young Vietnamese go-go girls do their stuff. Suddenly, I heard a very close, blunt, single shot that came from just a few rows of guys in front of me. The crowd made a hole and on the ground I saw a soldier with a gunshot wound to his head. The band stopped playing, MPs arrived immediately, and wrestled another soldier to the ground separating him from a .45 handgun. Some of the MPs shuffled off with the shooter in custody, others stood over the dead grunt and shouted out, "Party's over, get back to your hootches now." I never heard why the murder occurred but figured it was an REMF drug deal gone bad or some kind of love triangle turned violent. I wondered how the Army would classify that death; would it be accidental, KIA by incoming enemy rockets, or just plain old murder.

The following morning, I flew out to the final out-processing centre for northern and central grunts. There, I met Dunne and Benton, the grunts I had trained with. Benton had served his tour as a grunt in the American Division, and bragged about blowing away six dinks. Dunne, of course, had served in the Ranger Platoon with me, and had then been redeployed to the Americal Division where he served as a door gunner. They told me that our other bud, Cotter, had become a Jeep driver for his battalion commander and had gotten an early out. It was great to see those guys. We were going home, standing up.

J.J. arrived at the out-processing centre, high as usual. His DEROS was one day after mine but the system was flowing well and he had caught up to me. We all got new khaki uniforms to go home in and boarding passes for the aircraft. As J.J. and I approached our freedom bird, I noticed he was lollygagging, kinda holding back, as if he were deciding whether to board the aircraft or not. I stopped in my tracks, just metres from the ramp, and walked back to where J.J. was. He was trembling and appeared very frightened.

"J.J.," I said, "come on, man, don't do this, it's time to go home."

"I can't do it," he replied, "you go ahead, I'll fly out tomorrow."

"Please get your ass on that airplane," I pleaded.

He was in tears and hugged me. "I can't. I'll be okay, you go."

There was no way J.J. was leaving on that aircraft. I was torn, not knowing what to do. I reluctantly turned and boarded the aircraft, already feeling extreme guilt for abandoning one more comrade. I never saw J.J. again. I figured later that he was either holding drugs on his person and was worried about getting busted, or he wasn't holding and wanted to be. In a few months' time, the Army would begin administering urine tests to identify heroin addicts just prior to their departure. Those who tested positive would be housed in secure areas until they cleaned up, or whatever else happened. For many grunts, a lifelong addiction to heroin would be their legacy from Vietnam.

As the aircraft lifted off, some of the returnees applauded and cheered; they were mostly REMFs. The grunts were easy to spot. They were the quiet ones with sunken faces and damaged eyes.

6. FORT BENNING

In front of the Austin Healey, on the trip to Fort Benning, 1970.

We found ourselves back at Fort Lewis, Washington, where we were now the old grunts who entered the huge warehouse and exited all decked out in Class A uniforms with cool splashes of colour. We could see the new grunts entering the warehouse in Class As and exiting dressed in new, very green, jungle fatigues, complete with their names on them. They were being inserted. We were being extracted. They stared at us. We looked right beyond them.

It was our turn to be treated to the congratulatory steak dinner served by the new guys in the little white cottage. I found a seat at a table with three other guys who were REMF returnees. Our server approached the table. He was pale and seemed very, very stressed. One of the non-grunts asked him what his MOS was. The pale server replied that he was an infantryman. Salad and bread were served while we waited for our grilled-to-order steaks. The REMFs were getting cocky as they teased our pale grunt-to-be. As he delivered our steaks, a non-grunt said, "You know you're gonna die, huh kid?" The server burst into tears.

I jumped up from my seat, put an arm around the kid, and said, "You'll be okay, man, just chill out and you'll be okay." I looked at the non-grunts and said, "You guys are all fucked," then walked out without taking a bite of my steak.

I would be on leave for thirty days, before having to report to Fort Benning, Georgia, to finish off my required two years' active duty. I obeyed the order to wear my Class A uniform for the flight to Los Angeles. Full of conflicting emotions, I wondered: would loved ones accept me, could I handle the complex world of bright colour, could I hold it all together, would I lose it and go psycho, would I ever feel good inside again? I missed my fellow grunts, and our simple, easy-to-understand life in Vietnam. I was a mess.

I cheered up big-time when I exited the gate at Los Angeles International Airport and saw my entire family, Nancy and her entire family, and a group of close friends waiting for me. I immediately felt loved and welcomed.

There were hugs, kisses, handshakes, and back slaps; there were some tears but smiles outshined them. We all cruised up the San Diego Freeway to my family home in Granada Hills, where my mother served up a righteous homecoming meal of barbecued steak, potatoes, salad, bread, and my favourite, fresh fruit salad.

Nancy had kept her word and remained faithful in my absence. Her father had been a Marine in World War II and knew how devastating a "Dear John" letter could be to a soldier in a combat zone. He had made her promise him that she wouldn't do such a thing. I, too, had witnessed the effect of "Dear John" letters in Vietnam. To feel all the grunt deprivation and then be informed that you're no longer loved, was more than some could take.

I settled into my parents' home but felt very troubled. I found sleeping on a bed difficult. Occasionally I'd wake up on the floor covered in sweat, trembling from the nightmares. My grunt lingo did not fit in with my new world and I had to relearn an acceptable language that did not include the word "fuck" or the phrase "there it is." I was anxious to assimilate into civilian society but could not deny I felt a wistfulness and even a yearning for Vietnam.

I located my long ago abandoned surf Woody, only to discover that the new motor and tires had been ripped-off. It now looked to me like a brightly coloured circus wagon that didn't suit me any more. I figured I

needed some new wheels anyway, and so I purchased a
wrecked Austin Healey sports car for two hundred bucks.
I spent the days fixing up the Austin Healey in preparation for the long drive to Fort Benning, Georgia, where
I would serve my final six months in the Army.

Contrary to popular belief, returning enlisted vets did
not have buckets of cash that would have accumulated
while in Vietnam. My expensive R&R in Hawaii and the
three-day trip to Saigon had left me with $1,200 chump
change to purchase, insure, and fix up the Healey, as well
as party and get my ass to Fort Benning. There, I would
again be on the government payroll, waiting month to
month for the eagle to shit.

While on leave, Nancy and I went to a party at an
old friend's house. I was the only vet there. A young
American woman asked me to talk about Vietnam.

"America should pull out of there immediately," I
replied.

"How can you say that?" she said. "We've come so
far and victory is so close."

"Bullshit, victory is impossible, and if we get out now
at least the dying will stop."

This really angered her, and she started to attack me
personally. "Yeah, you just got back and you're fucked up."

I replied, "Maybe so, but if the current policy is
pursued, many more will be fucked up." She could not
accept what I was saying, and actually called me a "pinko
traitor" and accused me of undermining America's efforts

to save the free world. She wanted easy answers and reassurance, which I wasn't able to give her. For my part, I craved acceptance, respect, and compassion. I quickly learned to be a closet vet and not risk social suicide by talking about the war.

* * *

My thirty days of leave over, Nancy and I packed up the Austin Healey and headed for the Deep South. Nancy would make the road trip, then fly back to Los Angeles.

I duly reported to the reception centre at Fort Benning, where we were moved from station to station, and processed into our new units. Near the end of my first day there, an in-processing clerk approached me holding a broom in one hand.

"Here, sweep the floor," he said. "We're closing up."

"Fuck you, it's your floor, you sweep it." He did not outrank me and in my mind, was clearly fuckin' with the grunts.

He called his supervisor over, who arrived and asked what the problem was. The clerk told his staff sergeant boss how I had refused to sweep the floor. The staff sergeant must have recently been to a seminar designed to instruct lifers how to negotiate minor grunt uprisings as all he said to me was, "Move on, soldier."

I was looking for a fight, so I said, "Why the fuck am I getting fucked with?"

"Nobody's fuckin' with you," the staff sergeant replied. "Take it easy, he'll sweep the floor."

I now realized that my time left in the Army would be anything but relaxed.

The following day, all we returning grunts were loaded onto trucks for a tour of a facility the Army called "correctional custody." The trip to view correctional custody was the Army's way of saying, "If you fuck up, you will be sent here." The facility was a camp out in the middle of nowhere where the Army had tents set up. Each guest was assigned a sergeant who would be in charge of that correctee. It would be a one-on-one sentence of strict military discipline, beyond any I could have handled, to help us grunt returnees readjust. Our field trip to view CC was blatant intimidation by the Army, but it worked on me. I vowed to not get really out of control and get myself arrested, which proved to be a really tough vow to keep.

After a few days at the reception centre, we received our orders. I was assigned to Charlie Company First Battalion Fifty-Eight Infantry (Mechanized). My first thought was "A mechanized unit? I'm a ground pounder, I don't know the first thing about armoured personnel carriers." I was in the battalion for months before I finally realized why we used-up grunts had not been given early outs from the Army. We were unknowingly on standby to go into riot situations and wage war against our own people. Our battalion occupied really rundown World War II-era barracks way off the main post out in the boonies, where we trained in riot control tactics. Luckily, things did not line up for our deployment, but we were put on alert on several occasions. Once I figured out our secret role, I promised myself to go AWOL if the battalion were ever deployed, and deal with the consequences later.

Needless to say, the battalion was manned by an eclectic lot of grunt survivors. There were grunts from every corner of Vietnam, just a virtual goldmine of experience and knowledge. You'd think we brother grunts would have taken this opportunity to talk about the war and decompress. We did not, however, probably because we had no idea what to say to each other. The war was not over, the outcome was unknown, and our brothers were still being blown away. We just waited to see what would happen next.

They really should have kicked us grunts loose to go home and attempt to sort ourselves out. Guys who had impeccable records, were highly decorated, and had never been in trouble, now chose to go underground. Most didn't. I vowed to "maintain" and not fuck up but my bad attitude was impossible to hide.

As vet grunts, the Army used us as "aggressors" in mock battle situations to help train the newest of Rangers and officer candidates. One day, I got volunteered to be a gook sniper on an officer-training mission. We aggressors were trucked out to a mock Vietnamese village where we were to wait for the Americans to arrive. The instructor placed me on a trail and said, "The platoon will approach the village here. Your job is to wait until the platoon is on top of you, then fire up the point element quickly and vanish." I was armed with an M-14 and one magazine filled with blank ammo. The instructor added, "You've got several hours before the platoon gets here so kick back and wait."

I got into my role and decided to play the game to the max. I reconned the trail and found the kill zone I preferred. I located a paralleling trail that was just metres away from the trail that the officers-to-be would be approaching on. My paralleling trail had vegetation that provided excellent concealment. I poured water from my canteen onto the ground and created mud that I darkened my face with. I placed additional vegetation in front of my ambush position and waited.

I observed the platoon as they approached my kill zone. The platoon halted, the point element proned out right in my kill zone. I waited some more and eventually the platoon leader and his RTO low-crawled up to the point element. I opened fire destroying the pointman, his slack man, the platoon leader, and his RTO. The instructor yelled out, "Good job, aggressor, now identify yourself." I chuckled to myself, then ran down my paralleling trail to the position of the rear column. I again opened fire, destroying the rear element of the platoon. Still undetected, I ran back on my trail and fired my remaining rounds into the platoon at mid column. The instructor was clearly angry now. "Aggressor, that's enough; now identify yourself." I was out of ammo anyway so I stepped out of my concealment onto the ambushed trail. The officer candidates were pissed off about how unfairly I had acted.

I shrugged my shoulders and said, "Fair, Charlie don't play fair." The training platoon had been armed with M-16s and blanks as well. They had been so confused about what was happening, they had not even returned fire.

Duffy, my old battalion RTO bud who was at Fort Benning, and I would hang out on weekends and evenings to shoot the bull, play pool, and go into Columbus for a few beers. It didn't take long to realize that we were only semi-welcome anywhere we went. At this time, the U.S. Army, the war, the whole enchilada was on trial in America. Needless to say, we felt ostracized as well as powerless to effect change. We could not deny that we were Vietnam vets, because we were. We were guilty before any questions were asked.

Life in the old dilapidated World War II barracks could only be described as ghetto-like. The scene was depressing to say the least. As vet grunts, we were authorized to display our cool splashes of colour on our fatigues but few did. I wore the same old ratty fatigues I wore in basic training and AIT. I wore no Combat Infantryman Badge, no unit patch, and no rank insignia. I laundered my fatigues myself and never had them pressed or starched. In appearance, I resembled a wrinkled Sad Sack soldier who was really tired of playing the game.

Lifers, of course, hated us sloppy soldiers who were mocking the Army that they loved. The tension between lifers and draftees was indeed intense. The higher ups had been dealing with bad attitude for years and actually took some steps to not push us into mutiny. KP duty was contracted out to civilians because the Army had learned through experience that most of us would refuse the order to pull the dreaded detail. I had long ago quit saluting officers unless forced to do so. It was virtual war within the Army. Guys would commit minor infractions and be sent to CC where the bad attitude syndrome could intensify. Some would be given the choice of court martial or an Administrative Discharge. Many took the Administrative Discharge to be rid of the Army, not realizing that the bad paper would haunt them for the rest of their lives.

Occasionally Duffy, my old battalion RTO bud, and I would cruise down to the main post of Fort Benning to take in a movie or visit the PX. The main post seemed worlds away from our battalion area where we lived in virtual poverty. The Army had officer housing there that rivalled the mansions in Beverly Hills. The higher the rank, the more decadent the housing would be. We saw mansions that resembled southern plantation estates, complete with pillars, elaborate landscaping, and servants to keep everything perfect. It was obscene compared to

the squalor of low-ranking enlisted housing. The economic distance between the two groups was mind-boggling. In the jungles of Vietnam, rank had often meant
nothing. Experienced privates ran squads while sergeants
walked point or were machine gunners or RTOs.
Inexperienced platoon leaders often relinquished command to enlisted personnel who were more qualified to
lead. It was for us a survival thing. Survival was the point.

My plan had always been to simply do my time, and
slip through the cracks. Physically, my plan had worked,
but mentally, I was really suffering. All feelings had one
common thread: guilt. I felt guilty for going to Vietnam,
for allowing the Army to have my body, for reluctantly
pursuing a war I thought was nuts, for eventually abandoning my grunt brothers, and, mostly, for surviving
when others did not. I had not been blown away or
even slightly wounded when many others had. For
decades, I would blame myself for the very existence of
the war in Vietnam.

One day, we got volunteered to mark and score
targets at some high falutin' shootin' match the Army
was holding down on the main post. Snipers had come
from all corners of the Army to compete in this all-day
formal shoot-out. The trucks picked us up early so naturally the grunts were all pissing and moaning about the
hated Army, as was our habit. Our job was to pull, score,
and patch up the targets. Sounded simple enough, but
the drawback was that we had to work in the pit where

the targets were. Why couldn't they use guys that had never been shot at before? We had been shot at and didn't like it very much. They could have grabbed some new grunts that were at Benning for jump school or some fresh guys just out of AIT. But no, they had to use the old grunts.

Range officials instructed us by the numbers. We then assumed our work positions behind the pit. We were doing a good job and everything was going smoothly when some grunts thought they'd make it interesting and wave off incorrect scores just to see if they were paying attention. They were, with their scopes. The expert marksmen knew exactly where their last round had hit. Suddenly, after a volley of fire, I heard a loud shriek.

"Fuck, I'm hit. Jesus fuckin' Christ, I'm hit. Medic!"

A round had mysteriously ricocheted off something solid then flattened out, like a coin on a railroad track, then struck a grunt on the left forearm. Luckily, the velocity had been spent, and the grunt was only badly bruised. The wounded grunt grumbled off to an awaiting hospital room. We were close to mutiny, but a fast-talking lifer got us calmed down and the gunshots, scoring, and patching got underway again.

"Hey, mother fuckers, does he get a Purple Heart?"

"Yeah, at least give him a fuckin' medal."

"Or a steak dinner."

"Or a psycho pension."

We grumbled about that one for weeks.

* * *

The shorter I got, the more angry and vocal I got. I was goin' nuts with anger. One morning, Lieutenant Whitley entered our barracks early to make sure all us grunts were awake enough to make the morning formation. The morning formation was where we stood at attention, got fucked with, then received our orders and assignments for that day. I was hung over when Whitley said, "Brown, wake up."

"Fuck you," I immediately replied, thinking to myself, whoever you are, I'm sleepin' here. Whitley was an officer who had just finished Officer Candidate School and was assigned to the battalion to get command experience prior to his Vietnam tour. It wasn't his fault, he didn't write the rules, so he was just doing his job when he reported the incident to Captain Brown, our company commander. I was ordered to report to the orderly room.

I thought to myself, "What's the big deal? All I said was 'Fuck you.' It don't mean nothin'." I had actually gotten dressed and reported to the morning formation without being late, but Whitley and Brown were anxious to teach me a lesson. I had three weeks left in the U.S.

Army and figured I'd learned all of the lessons. Just goes to show you. It's not over till it's over.

Captain Brown's interrogation did not go well for me. I should have put on a clean set of fatigues, polished my boots, shined my brass belt buckle, gotten a haircut, and adjusted my attitude but I didn't. I figured, "Fuck this shit, kick me loose please. I really just wanna go home." Apparently, the sight of me offended Captain Brown as he barked out, "You're not out of the Army yet, Brown, and if you don't soon salute me, I will see to it that you spend six months in the stockade."

I had wanted to just talk things out guy to guy, but in a lapse of good decision-making, I hadn't saluted an officer. I forced myself to salute, then stood ill at ease when ordered to do so. Captain Brown sat at his official desk, while the first shirt stood at parade rest in the doorway to the Captain's office. It was not a friendly powwow but rather a formal gathering to investigate my attitude.

I said to the CO, "Does he need to be here?" referring to the first shirt.

"Yes, he does," the CO replied. "Now shut up, Brown. I'm in charge here."

"Look, I only got three weeks left," I said. "I've been a good trooper, I've gone along with the program, and now it's time for me to go home."

"Did you say 'fuck you' to Lieutenant Whitley?" he asked.

"Well, yeah, I believe I did."

"Brown, you said it yourself, you still have three weeks, and in that three weeks, I will personally teach you some respect. You are confined to your barracks during off-duty hours, you will get an acceptable military haircut, and you will shine your boots and polish your brass. You will report to the battalion commander at 1100 hours this Saturday, and I would hardly describe you as a good trooper. Now get out."

Aw shit, I thought, I really screwed this one up. Way to go, idiot. I resigned myself to giving in and shined everything. I reluctantly got an Army haircut, and started stressin' about my Saturday rendezvous with the colonel. I knew if I blew this meeting swift military punishment would quickly follow.

On Saturday, I was punctual and stepped smartly to the front of the Colonel's desk doing everything by the numbers and feigning respect to an acceptable level. The Colonel was businesslike in approach. I'm sure he would have rather been home with his family on a Saturday. The Colonel quickly attacked to test my attitude.

"Brown, is that your best set of fatigues?"

They weren't, but they were the cleanest. I replied, "Yes, sir." I was surprised by his next question.

"How many sets of fatigues do you have, Brown?"

"Four, sir."

"And what is the disposition of those fatigues?"

"Well, I'm wearing this set, two are at the laundry, and one set is in my locker, sir."

"How old are those fatigues, Brown?"

"They're my basic training fatigues, sir."

"Well, it shows. Did you say 'fuck you' to Lieutenant Whitley?"

"Yes, sir, but I regret it."

"Lieutenant Whitley is an officer of the United States Army and you have shown disrespect to him, and by doing so, to every officer in this Army. Do you understand that, Brown?"

I wanted to say, "Fuck you too; where's my respect?" but knew the Colonel would not hesitate to jail me. I replied, "Yes, sir, I do."

"Did you make it to the formation on time?"

"Yes, sir, I did."

"Do you think you can conduct yourself as a soldier in the United States Army for the next three weeks?"

"Yes, sir."

"Due to the fact that you were not late for the formation and because, from what I understand, legally a person is not responsible for what he says when just awakened, I'm willing to overlook this incident. Brown, we'll be watching you. Don't screw up."

"I won't." Pause. "Sir."

They watched me for sure, but I hunkered down and kept my mouth shut. I knew that if I went to the stockade that I'd lose it and become institutionalized forever. I could smell freedom.

* * *

I was discharged from the U.S. Army 12 May 1971. One month before, Vietnam veterans against the war had participated in a huge rally in Washington, as two hundred thousand demonstrators marched on the capital. The vets chanted, "Bring our Brothers Home." After all we'd been through, grunts were still gettin' their shit blowed away in the mud.

EPILOGUE

t's not easy being a Vietnam veteran, especially a Canadian one. After my discharge, I returned to Los Angeles figuring that my future was there. I had no trade other than soldiering and soon discovered that I was two years behind those who didn't go to war. I had some serious catching up to do.

I took a motorcycle repair course and in January 1972 got a job as a mechanic. Motorcycles were my life for the next couple of years, as I tinkered on them at work and at home, and even raced them on weekends. In 1973, Nancy and I were married.

I still suffered silently from my memories of the war. I felt that something was missing, and I thought perhaps it was action or the opportunity to be part of something bigger. In 1974, I joined the Los Angeles Police Department, and, as a requirement of the job, took on American citizenship. I worked the streets of Los Angeles for a few years, but soon realized that a career in law enforcement was not what I wanted or needed.

In May 1977 Nancy and I moved to Canada as landed immigrants. We purchased a ninety-acre farm in Farrellton, Quebec, located ten miles north of Wakefield, my mother's birthplace. We quickly learned "back to the land" skills and soon established a small mixed farming operation that we were both proud of. Between income from the farm and money I earned in the winter working at a local ski resort, we were able to pay the bills and grow slowly.

Nancy and I tried to have children, but found that we couldn't. In 1981, after a complicated and lengthy adoption process, we adopted our son, Jason. I fell in love with him instantly.

The farming went well, as Nancy and I became accustomed to living and working in the cold north. At times, I could not have been happier. The land and animals taught us much about the circle of life and about ourselves. Inside, though, I was still troubled by the war. I thought about Vietnam daily, and I continued to have nightmares and flashbacks.

While working at the local ski resort one winter, I met Rosanne Pommier, a fellow employee who tended bar. Initially, we were only friends, but as time passed, we became attracted to each other and began a relationship. When I told her that I was a Vietnam vet, she offered to be my nurse. Soon my love for Rose was so strong, that it led me to leave the farm and Nancy. Nancy and I divorced, and eventually Rose and I moved to the farm. Nancy still lives in the area with our son, Jason. She operates a successful business, and we remain friends.

In 1989, Rose and I had our first child, Michael. Later that year we made a trip to Las Vegas and got married.

In 1990, my father, who had taken up flying later in life, and who was a well-known aviator in Los Angeles, was killed when his plane crashed. Prior to his death, my parents, Rose, and I had gone to see the movie *Platoon*. As we exited the theatre, my Dad said to me, "I had no idea." I told him that it was okay, not many people did. From then on, he accepted me fully as a combat veteran and our relationship flourished.

In February 1995, on a day of freezing rain and black skies, I was standing outside when a powerful gust of wind from the south lifted our cattle barn off its foundation and dropped it in a heap. It was as if every muzzle flash from the war had been directed at it. Instead of being defeated by it, I took it as a signal for change. I sold the livestock, and quit farming.

That summer, our son Nicholas was born, adding to our joy!

Around this time, my friend Phil Nolan, a news cameraman, interviewed me in relation to a story about a group of American Vietnam vets who were raising money to build a memorial in Ottawa to Canadian Vietnam vets. (The Canadian government refused to accept the memorial, explaining that Canada had not been officially involved in the war. Eventually, the city of Windsor, Ontario came forward with an offer to be home to the memorial. Today, the "North Wall," inscribed with the names of Canadians who died in Vietnam, stands in a park on Windsor's waterfront.) Through Phil, I met Lee Hitchins, president of the Canadian Vietnam Veterans Ottawa. His first words to me were, "Welcome home, brother." I have been active with the CVVO ever since.

Our daughter, Jackie, was born in November 1997. I had never felt so complete and energized. I immediately went to work on this book. I stayed up late at night with Jackie, writing, reliving my war experience while feeding her bottles every three hours.

As I wrote, it became obvious that I had issues to resolve. With much prodding from Rose, I sought professional help and started to visit Dr. Gerasimos I. Kambites in Ottawa, who treats as well as suffers from Post Traumatic Stress Disorder (PTSD).

* * *

If you know a veteran, let him speak. You may not like what he has to say, but he is worthy of your effort. In my mind, he fought for the freedom of everyone.

Veterans, come out of your bunkers and be with your people. Attend the meetings and gatherings. We got through the war together – we can help each other now.

As for me, it's time to get on with life's biggest challenge, child rearing. I embrace my children and our future.

GLOSSARY

AO	Area of Operation.
Article 15	Summary disciplinary judgement of a soldier by his commanding officer, which could result in fines, loss of rank, extra duty, or confinement in stockade. No court martial would be involved.
ARVN	Army of the Republic of [South] Vietnam.
AWOL	Absent Without Leave.
Basecamp	Base of operations. The size of basecamps varied greatly.
Blueline	Slang for a stream.

Bowl	Pipe in which marijuana was smoked.
Butter bar	Second lieutenant. Based on the insignia, a single gold bar.
Charlie	Slang for enemy soldier.
CIB	Combat Infantryman Badge. Awarded to infantrymen who saw combat. No other MOS could wear it.
Clacker	Firing device for triggering claymore mines and other electrically initiated demolitions.
Claymore	Arc-shaped anti-personnel land mine, which when detonated produced a directionalized, fan-shaped pattern of fragments.
Clusterfuck	Any gathering of soldiers where order and security are not present.
CO	Commanding Officer or Conscientious Objector.
CP	Command Position.
C-rations	Canned food, provided by the Army.
Crotch	Slang for the Marine Corps.
CS gas	Tear gas.
DEROS	Date Eligible Return from Overseas.
Dew	Grunt slang for marijuana. From Vietnamese word for love.
DI	Drill instructor.
Didi mau	To leave or depart. As a command, it meant to leave in a hurry.

DMZ	Demilitarized Zone. The area between North and South Vietnam at the 17th parallel.
Dustoff	Air medical evacuation.
E-4	Corporal or specialist fourth class.
E-5	Sergeant or specialist fifth class.
E-6	Staff sergeant or specialist sixth class.
Eleven Bravo	Army MOS designation for Light Weapons Infantryman.
Firebase	Remote base with the purpose of supplying grunts with artillery and mortar fire at any given time. Firebases came and went. Some were abandoned after being overrun by the enemy.
First shirt	First sergeant, the senior enlisted man in a company.
FNG	Fucking new guy or funny new guy.
Frag (noun)	Fragmentation grenade thrown by hand.
Frag (verb)	To murder an officer with a frag.
Free fire zone	An area where we could open fire freely, without restriction. If it moved, we could shoot it.
FSU	Forward supply unit.
Ground pounder	Infantryman.
Grunt	Infantryman.
Hootch	Any structure, large or small, built as protection from the elements.

Hump	To travel on foot, to march or walk.
Jungle penetrator	Device lowered through jungle canopies by steel cable from dustoff ships to extract wounded soldiers.
KIA	Killed-in-action.
Kill zone	Area of ambush where enemy was allowed to enter in order to maximize kills.
Klick	One kilometre.
KP	Kitchen police. Clean-up and preparation work in the kitchen.
La Dai	Vietnamese for Come Here.
LAW	Light anti-tank weapon.
LBJ	Long Binh Jail.
Leg	Slang for walking grunts, as opposed to paratroopers, or airborne grunts.
Lifer	Career soldier.
Loach	Light observation helicopter.
Lurp rations	Dehydrated rations. Slang for LRP or Long Range Patrol.
LZ	Landing Zone.
MOS	Military Occupational Specialty.
NCO	Non-Commissioned Officer.
NDP	Night Defensive Position.
NLF	National Liberation Front, a Vietcong Organization.
NVA	North Vietnamese Army.

Paradise	Slang for Vietnam.
Punji stick	Sharp bamboo stakes often coated with excrement to wound and infect the feet of GIS. Usually concealed in shallow camouflaged pits.
Rat fuck	A delay in receiving supplies or an extension of an operation. Term used generally to refer to being messed with by the Army.
REMF	Rear echelon mother fucker. Slang used by grunts to disparagingly refer to rear-area personnel.
RTO	Radio telephone operator.
Ruck	Rucksack.
Sapper	A highly motivated enemy soldier who specialized in infiltrating American perimeters and killing GIS, usually with satchel charges.
Shake 'n' bake	Derogatory slang for a non-commissioned officer straight out of sergeant school.
Short	To have little time left in the Army or in Vietnam.
Skag	Heroin.
Slack man	Second man in snake-like column.
Stand down	Refers to when a unit leaves an AO to get a rest or change locations.

Steelpot	Army helmet.
Thump gunner	Grunt that carried the M-79 grenade launcher.
VC	Vietcong.
Vietnamization	The U.S. government's plan to equip and train ARVNs so that U.S. soldiers could be gradually withdrawn from Vietnam.

ACKNOWLEDGEMENTS

Special thanks to my close friend Global TV camerman and Canadian military history buff Phil Nolan, who encouraged me to tell my story. Thanks, too, to Phil's dad, Brian Nolan, a veteran of the Korean War and an author of several military books. Brian read the manuscript when it was still in long-hand and half-completed, and told me to "keep moving forward, you only have ten more yards to go."

Eternal gratitude to Dr. Gerasimos I. Kambites in Ottawa, who encouraged me to seek peace of mind. Eternal love to my sister Ginny, whose tireless work to type and organize the manuscript brought us closer than I had imagined possible.

Special thanks to my editor, Rudy Mezzetta, whose work and sound suggestions helped me to shape the manuscript into a book, and to my copyeditor, Lynn Schellenberg, who smoothed out all the edges. Thanks also goes to Doug Gibson, Jonathan Webb, Lesley Horlick, Adrienne Guthrie, Ingrid Paulson, and everyone else at McClelland & Stewart who helped make this book possible.

A huge thank-you to Peter Kent, who generously provided the insightful introduction for this book.

Much respect and love to Ottawa-area vets Denis Labrecque, Davin McLaughlin, Eric Walsh, and Bob McFall, who supported me through the process of writing. We were all in combat in Vietnam at around the same time, and now we get together regularly just so we can be with our own.

But most of all, thanks to my family, who never gave up on me, and especially my wife, Rosanne, who rekindled in me optimism, love, and trust in my spirit.